The 20 Minute Keto Diet Recipe Book

The Easy Way to Get Back in Shape Starting
Your New Healthy Lifestyle With Affordable, Quick & Tasty
Low-Carb Recipes for Beginners & Busy People

Amanda Lloyd

TABLE OF CONTENT

Introduction

This recipe book was created for individuals who are interested in the ketogenic diet but do not enjoy cooking, do not have the time to prepare elaborate meals, and desire a more straightforward way of living.

With the help of the keto diet, getting into shape in a relatively short period of time has never been simpler.

You will learn how to cook foods that are not only delicious but also healthy, while adhering to all of the requirements of the keto diet, in less than twenty minutes.

Having stated that, let's take a quick look at the ketogenic diet and see what it entails.

To begin, allow me to tell you that the ketogenic diet is one of the most successful and most famous diets, specifically for its favourable outcomes both in terms of health as well as, most importantly, for those who want to lose weight and body fat in a short amount of time.

The ketogenic diet is a nutritional plan that is in reality based on reducing the amount of carbs consumed throughout the course of the day. This "forces" the body to manufacture the glucose that is essential for living on its own, and it also "forces" the body to increase the amount of energy that it consumes from the fat that is contained in the adipose tissue. Both of these processes are necessary for survival.

As a consequence of this, the ketogenic diet is also commonly known as a low-carb diet.

The phrase "diet that creates ketone bodies" refers to the metabolic residue left over from the creation of energy. A ketogenic diet is one such diet.

Ketone bodies, which are formed on a regular basis in very small numbers and can be eliminated from the body relatively simply through the kidneys and the lungs, reach an elevated level when a ketogenic diet is followed. Ketone bodies can be eliminated from the body quite simply through the kidneys and the lungs.

In the simplest terms imaginable, what are some of the benefits that come along with following this diet? A nutritional plan known as the ketogenic diet is characterised by the following qualities and characteristics:

➢ High in protein content, despite the absolute amount (in grammes) being more commonly medium - keep in mind that the liver can employ neo glucogenic amino acids to create glucose

➢ Containing a high percentage of lipids.

➢ As you can see, the meal plans and recipes will adhere to these dietary standards that have just been outlined.

After we have finished presenting it, we will quickly discuss how the keto diet can help people shed unwanted pounds.

You should be aware that in order to initiate ketosis, you are required to adhere to a ketogenic diet that is designed around a set of principles that must be followed religiously.

The ketogenic diet requires a minimal reduction in the daily amount of carbs, which are an absolute adversary of ketosis. This ensures that you will be able to lose weight while following the diet.

It is imperative to reduce the daily dose, which should not exceed 20–50 mg of net carbohydrates per day. Net carbohydrates are determined by deducting the amount of dietary fibre from total carbohydrates. Therefore, it is recommended to cut back on the consumption of sugary beverages, carbonated drinks, and fruit juices as much as possible. Both coffee and tea are allowed on the keto diet; however, none of these beverages should have any added sugars. On the other hand, increasing the number of lipids that are burned is something that should be done.

For fats to be ingested regularly and make up 70% of the diet that is selected, the majority of them need to be healthy fats.

➢ The avocado and avocado oil are among the most appropriate options

➢ Chocolate

➢ Extra-virgin olive oil

- ➢ Dried fruit (including almonds, pistachios, walnuts, and cashews)
- ➢ Eggs, butter, and cheese (both of which contain animal fat)
- ➢ Vegetable oils (including olive, sunflower, flax, and coconut)
- ➢ Fish (including tuna and salmon, as well as cod, plaice, and haddock)
- ➢ Hemp, chia, and flax seeds.

Instead, you should try to steer clear of foods that contain trans fat, such as those that are industrially manufactured, fried foods, and processed meats, particularly if these items contain hydrogenated oils.

On the other hand, protein ought to account for thirty percent of the diet. This is because, when there is an excess of them, they undergo a process known as gluconeogenesis, in which they are converted into glucose rather than ketones.

On the other hand, if they are of excellent quality and have a high biological value, like whey isolate, they are beneficial to the process of keeping muscle mass.

It is of the utmost importance to adhere to the dietary plan that is presented by the ketogenic diet throughout each and every meal, beginning with breakfast and continuing through supper, as well as lunch and snacks.

The latter is absolutely necessary for preventing and treating hunger episodes. Midway during the morning or afternoon, it is recommended that you snack on walnuts, a piece of parmesan cheese, or a fruit of your choosing.

As soon as you wake up, it is also beneficial to consume a glass of warm water with lemon, and during the day, it is recommended that you consume at least two litres of water.

Last but not least, you must engage in at least ten minutes of moderate but continuous physical activity each day.

This time should be increased as the body becomes accustomed to the new sources of energy, which are ketones, in fact.

Because they are low in carbohydrates and high in fibre, green vegetables are an essential component of a ketogenic diet. In addition to making you feel more full, a keto diet allows you to consume the optimal quantity of essential micronutrients like vitamins and mineral salts.

Following an explanation of how following a keto diet can assist with weight loss, the next section of this guide will provide one hundred recipes that adhere to the guidelines of the keto diet and are both delicious and satisfying.

The recipes will be organised as follows: Breakfast; Main Courses (including Meat, Poultry, Fish, and Seafood); Salads; Soups (both warm and cold); Snacks; and Desserts.

Recipes

Breakfast

Avocado and salmon on lettuce

2 servings I Calories 400
Nutritional values: carbs 2.8g, protein 21g, fat 29 g

Ingredients
- ✓ 1 avocado, sliced
- ✓ 100 gr of lettuce
- ✓ 200 gr of smoked salmon
- ✓ 8 cherry tomatoes
- ✓ 4 tbsp of mayonnaise
- ✓ Oregano to taste
- ✓ Pepper to taste

Directions
- ➢ Peel, pit and slice the avocado.
- ➢ Wash and rinse the lettuce.
- ➢ Wash, dry and slice the tomatoes.
- ➢ Spread the lettuce on the plate, add the salmon, tomatoes, mayonnaise, oregano and pepper.

Avocado with bacon and eggs

2 servings I nutritional values: calories 330, carbs 5g, protein 18g, fat 32g

Ingredients
- ✓ 1 avocado
- ✓ 2 eggs

✓ 40 gr of bacon
✓ ½ shallot
✓ 1 lime
✓ Salt and pepper to taste
✓ Olive oil to taste

Directions
➢ Wash and dry the avocado, cut it in half, remove the stone and remove some of the pulp with a spoon.
➢ Sprinkle the avocado shells with the lime juice.
➢ Put the avocado shells in a baking pan and season with oil, salt, and pepper.
➢ Shell the eggs in the centre of the avocado and sprinkle with the diced bacon.
➢ Put the baking pan in the oven and cook at 200 °c for 12 minutes.
➢ Once cooked, take the baking pan out of the oven, put the avocados with eggs and bacon on the plates and serve.

Avocado stuffed with cherry tomatoes and cheese

2 servings I nutritional values: calories 265, carbs 6g, protein 8g, fat 19g

Ingredients
✓ 1 avocado
✓ 50 gr of soft fresh cheese
✓ 50 gr of cherry tomatoes
✓ 4 basil leaves
✓ Apple cider vinegar to taste
✓ Salt and pepper to taste
✓ Olive oil to taste

Directions

1. Wash and dry the avocado. Cut it in half and remove the stone.
2. With a spoon take some of the pulp and put it in a bowl.
3. Wash the cherry tomatoes and cut them into cubes. Also cut the cheese into cubes.
4. Put the cherry tomatoes and cheese in the bowl with the avocado pulp.
5. Season with oil, salt, pepper, and apple cider vinegar and mix well.
6. Fill the avocado shells with the filling.
7. Decorate with the washed and dried basil leaves, put the stuffed avocado on plates and serve.

Avocado stuffed with salmon

2 servings I Calories: 278
Nutritional values: carbs: 4 gr; protein: 11 gr; fat: 22 gr.

Ingredients
✓ 1 ripe avocado
✓ 100 gr of smoked salmon
✓ 1 tomato
✓ ½ lemon
✓ Soy sauce to taste
✓ Chopped pistachios to taste
✓ Salt and pepper to taste
✓ Olive oil to taste

Directions
➢ Wash and dry the avocado, cut it in half and remove the stone.
➢ Take the pulp with the help of a spoon and put it in a bowl.
➢ Wash the tomato, cut it into cubes and put it in the bowl with the avocado.

> ➢ Cut the salmon into small pieces and place in the bowl with the avocado pulp.
> ➢ Add the lemon juice, salt, pepper, soy sauce and a little oil and mix well.
> ➢ Put the avocado shells on two plates and add the filling.
> ➢ Sprinkle with chopped pistachios and serve.

Baked eggs

2 servings I Calories: 270
Nutritional values: carbs: 7 gr; protein: 12 gr; fat: 22 gr

Ingredients
- ✓ 4 eggs
- ✓ 300 gr of peeled tomato
- ✓ 1 clove of garlic
- ✓ Dried oregano to taste
- ✓ Chopped parsley to taste
- ✓ Salt and pepper to taste
- ✓ Olive oil to taste

Directions
- ➢ Brush a baking dish with olive oil and put the tomato inside.
- ➢ Shell the eggs and put them on the tomato. Sprinkle with peeled and minced garlic.
- ➢ Sprinkle with salt, pepper and dried oregano and put the baking dish in the oven. Cook at 200 ° c for 15 minutes.
- ➢ After 15 minutes, take the baking dish out of the oven. Put the eggs and tomatoes on the plates, sprinkle with the chopped parsley and serve.

Bowls of Greek yoghurt and raspberries

2 servings I Calories: 330
Nutritional values: carbs: 7 gr; protein: 4 gr; fat: 12 gr

Ingredients
- ✓ 200 gr of Greek yoghurt
- ✓ 100 gr of raspberries
- ✓ 1 vanilla bean
- ✓ 1 tsp of stevia
- ✓ 2 tbsp of chopped pistachios

Directions
- ➢ Wash and dry the raspberries and then cut them into small pieces.
- ➢ Put the Greek yoghurt in a bowl and add the stevia and vanilla and mix well.
- ➢ Put some yoghurt on the bottom of two bowls.
- ➢ Place the raspberries on top and then cover with the rest of the yoghurt.
- ➢ Sprinkle with chopped pistachios and serve.

Cougette rolls

2 servings I Calories 198
Nutritional values: carbs 5.8 g, protein 12g, fat 13g

- ✓ 1 medium courgette
- ✓ 200 gr of ricotta cheese
- ✓ Fresh parsley
- ✓ Oregano, to taste
- ✓ Salt and pepper
- ✓ EVO

Directions:
- ➢ Wash and dry the courgette.
- ➢ Cut lengthwise the courgette.
- ➢ Spread the ricottas cheese onto each courgettes slice. Spread oregano and fresh parsley to

taste, a pinch of salt and pepper.

➤ Roll up the slices.
➤ Season with a drizzle of EVO before serving.

Eggs and spinach

2 servings I Calories: 307
Nutritional values: carbs: 7 gr; protein:10 gr; fat:25 gr

Ingredients
- ✓ 240 gr of spinach
- ✓ 2 eggs
- ✓ ½ clove
- ✓ 30 gr of butter
- ✓ 50 ml of cooking cream
- ✓ Salt and pepper to taste

Directions
➤ Wash and dry the spinach.
➤ Melt the butter in a pan and then add the garlic. Brown it and then add the spinach.
➤ Cook for 10 minutes, season with salt and pepper and then add the cooking cream.
➤ Shell the eggs on the spinach and cover the pan with a lid.
➤ Cook for 5 minutes, then turn off.
➤ Put the eggs and spinach on the plates and serve.

Eggs stuffed with avocado

2 servings I Calories: 245
Nutritional values: carbs: 3 gr; protein: 12 gr; fat: 19 gr

Ingredients
- ✓ 4 eggs

- ✓ 1 small ripe avocado
- ✓ ½ clove of garlic
- ✓ 1 tbsp of lemon juice
- ✓ Chopped chives to taste
- ✓ Salt and pepper to taste

Directions
➤ Put the eggs in a saucepan and cover them with water. Bring to a boil and continue cooking for another 8 minutes. After cooking, pass them under cold water, shell them and cut them in half.
➤ Take the egg yolks, put them in a bowl and mash them with a fork.
➤ Peel the avocado, remove the stone, and put the pulp in a bowl. Mash the avocado pulp with a fork. Add the lemon juice, the chopped chives, salt and pepper and mix. Now add the yolk and mix everything well.
➤ Put the eggshells on two plates. Fill the eggs with the filling and serve.

Fruit salad of strawberries and avocado

2 servings I Calories: 188
Nutritional values: carbs: 9 gr; protein: 2 gr; fat: 12 gr

Ingredients
- ✓ 200 gr of strawberries
- ✓ 1 small ripe avocado
- ✓ 1 lemon
- ✓ 1 tsp of sweetener powder

Directions
➤ Wash and dry the strawberries, cut them into small pieces and put them in a bowl.
➤ Peel the avocado, remove the stone, and then cut it into cubes and

put it in the bowl with the strawberries.

➤ Add the sweetener and the filtered lemon juice and mix well.

➤ Put the bowl in the fridge and let it rest for 1 hour.

➤ After the hour, take the bowl from the fridge, divide the fruit salad into two bowls and serve.

Keto pancakes with strawberries

2 servings I Calories: 404
Nutritional values: carbs: 4 gr; protein: 14 gr; fat: 35 gr

Ingredients
✓ 2 eggs
✓ 100 ml of fresh cream
✓ 100 gr of cottage cheese
✓ 30 gr of strawberries
✓ 1 tsp of stevia powder

Directions
➤ Break the eggs into a bowl. Add the cottage cheese and stevia powder and mix well, until you get a homogeneous mixture.

➤ Put the mixture aside and let it rest for 10 minutes.

➤ Meanwhile, put the cream in a bowl and whip it until stiff peaks.

➤ Wash and dry the strawberries and then cut them into slices.

➤ After 10 minutes, heat a non-stick pan, pour a little batter, and cook for 3 minutes per side. Repeat the operation until the ingredients are finished.

➤ Once cooked, divide the pancakes on plates, add the cream and strawberries and serve.

Mint frittata

2 servings I Calories: 303
Nutritional values: carbs:2 gr; protein: 21 gr; fat: 24 gr

Ingredients
✓ 4 eggs
✓ 12 mint leaves
✓ 100 gr of cheddar
✓ 2 tablespoons of grated parmesan cheese
✓ 50 gr of bacon cut into cubes
✓ Salt and pepper to taste
✓ Olive oil to taste

Directions
➤ Wash and dry the mint leaves and then chop them.

➤ Break the eggs into a bowl. Beat them with a fork and then add salt, pepper, parmesan, bacon, mint, and diced cheddar.

➤ Stir until you get a homogeneous mixture.

➤ Heat a little olive oil in a pan and, when it is hot, pour the mixture inside.

➤ Cook for 7 minutes, then turn the omelette over and cook for another 8 minutes.

➤ After cooking, turn off, divide the omelette in two, put it on plates and serve.

Mushroom omelette

2 servings I Calories: 259
Nutritional values: carbs: 3 gr; protein: 13 gr; fat: 16 gr

Ingredients
✓ 3 eggs
✓ 150 gr of champignon mushrooms

- ✓ 1 clove of garlic
- ✓ 40 gr of grated parmesan cheese
- ✓ Chopped parsley to taste
- ✓ Olive oil to taste
- ✓ Salt and pepper to taste

Directions

- ➤ Clean the mushrooms, rinse them under running water and dry them well. Remove the final part of the mushrooms and cut the rest into thin slices.
- ➤ Peel the garlic clove, chop it and then brown it in a pan with a drizzle of hot olive oil.
- ➤ Add the mushrooms, season with salt and pepper, mix and cook for 10 minutes. After 10 minutes, turn off and temporarily set aside.
- ➤ Break the eggs into a bowl. Add salt, pepper and parmesan and beat them with a fork.
- ➤ Add the mushrooms and parsley and mix well.
- ➤ Heat a drizzle of oil in a non-stick pan. Pour the mixture, cook for 6 minutes, and then turn the omelette. Continue cooking for another 6 minutes and then turn off.
- ➤ Divide the omelette into two parts, put it on plates and serve.

Onion omelette

2 servings I Calories 130
Nutritional values: carbs 0.8 g, protein 9 g, fat 8 g

Ingredients:
- ✓ 4 medium eggs
- ✓ 2 medium white onions, sliced
- ✓ Fresh parsley, to taste
- ✓ 6 mint leaves

- ✓ 25 gr of parmesan cheese, grated
- ✓ Salt and pepper
- ✓ EVO

Directions:
- ➤ In a bowl combine the eggs with the onions, parsley (chopped), mint leaves (chopped), parmesan cheese, salt and pepper.
- ➤ Pour the mixture in a pan with 2 tbsp of EVO and let it cook 5-6 minutes for each side.

Parsley omelette

2 servings I Calories: 289
Nutritional values: carbs: 3 gr; protein: 21 gr; fat: 22 gr

Ingredients
- ✓ 3 eggs
- ✓ 60 gr of grated cheese
- ✓ 30 ml of milk
- ✓ 1 tbsp of chopped parsley
- ✓ Salt and pepper to taste
- ✓ Olive oil to taste

Directions
- ➤ Break the eggs into a bowl. Add salt, pepper, cheese, and milk.
- ➤ Mix well with a fork and then add the parsley.
- ➤ Stir until the parsley is completely incorporated.
- ➤ Heat a drizzle of oil in a pan and, when hot, pour the mixture.
- ➤ Cook for 5 minutes then, with the help of a lid, turn the omelette.
- ➤ Cook for another 5 minutes, then turn off, divide the omelette into two plates and serve.

Scrambled eggs and bacon

2 Servings I Calories: 334
Nutritional values: carbs: 1 gr; protein: 22 gr; fat: 28 gr

Ingredients
- ✓ 4 eggs
- ✓ 4 slices of bacon
- ✓ 50 gr of grated cheddar
- ✓ Salt and pepper to taste

Directions
- ➢ Shell the eggs in a bowl and add salt, pepper, and cheddar. Mix well until you get a homogeneous mixture.
- ➢ Heat a non-stick pan and place the bacon slices.
- ➢ Cook for two minutes on each side and then remove the bacon from the pan.
- ➢ Now pour the eggs into the same pan where you cooked the bacon.
- ➢ Cook for 4 minutes, stirring constantly.
- ➢ Now put the bacon on the plates, add the eggs and serve.

Scrambled eggs with cherry tomatoes

2 servings I Calories: 225
Nutritional values: carbs: 6 gr; protein: 13 gr; fat: 17 gr

Ingredients
- ✓ 50 gr of cherry tomatoes
- ✓ 3 eggs
- ✓ 50 gr of grated cheddar
- ✓ 20 gr of black olives
- ✓ 1 tbsp of chopped onion
- ✓ Salt and pepper to taste

- ✓ Olive oil to taste

Directions
- ➢ Wash the cherry tomatoes and cut them into cubes.
- ➢ Heat some oil in a pan and put the onion to cook for 2 minutes.
- ➢ Add the cherry tomatoes and cook for another 2 minutes.
- ➢ Break the eggs directly into the pan and mix continuously with a hand whisk for 2 minutes.
- ➢ Now add the chopped black olives and the cheddar and mix for another 2 minutes.
- ➢ Season with salt and pepper, stir for a few more seconds and then turn off.
- ➢ Divide the scrambled eggs into two plates and serve.

Scrambled eggs with cooked ham

2 servings I Calories: 396
Nutritional values: carbs: 2 gr; protein: 23 gr; fat: 32 gr

Ingredients
- ✓ 4 eggs
- ✓ 20 g of butter
- ✓ 50 g of cooked ham
- ✓ 2 tablespoons of cooking cream
- ✓ 25 grams of grated cheddar
- ✓ Salt and pepper to taste

Directions
- ➢ Melt the butter in a non-stick pan. Cut the ham into small pieces, put it in the pan and sauté for 1 minute.
- ➢ Shell the eggs directly into the pan and add salt and pepper.

➢ Stir with a manual whisk, cook for 2 minutes, and then add the cooking cream.

➢ Cook for 2 minutes and then add the cheddar. Stir and cook until the cheese has completely melted.

➢ After cooking, turn off, put the scrambled eggs on the plates and serve.

Shot glasses with strawberries and Greek yoghurt

2 servings I Calories: 209
Nutritional values: carb: 9 gr; protein: 16 gr; fat: 7 gr

Ingredients
✓ 150 gr of fresh strawberries
✓ 150 gr of Greek yoghurt
✓ 1 tsp of stevia powder
✓ 6 mint leaves

Directions
➢ Wash and dry the strawberries. Cut them in half and put them in the blender glass.

➢ Add the stevia, operate the blender, and blend the strawberries until you get a homogeneous mixture.

➢ Put the strawberry cream in a bowl and leave to rest in the fridge for 1 hour.

➢ After the hour, take 6 small glasses and put the Greek yoghurt on the bottom and pour over the strawberry cream.

➢ Add a mint leaf, washed and dried in each small glass and serve.

Smoked salmon and avocado with lime and soy sauce

2 servings I Calories: 350
Nutritional values: carbs: 3 gr; protein: 18 gr; fat: 25 gr

Ingredients
✓ 100 gr of smoked salmon
✓ 1 avocado
✓ 1 lime
✓ 1 tbsp of soy sauce
✓ Olive oil to taste
✓ Pepper to taste

Directions
➢ Peel the avocado, remove the stone, and then cut the pulp into slices.

➢ Put the salmon slices on a serving dish.

➢ Add the avocado slices.

➢ Put in a bowl and add oil, soy sauce, lime juice and pepper and mix well.

➢ Pour the emulsion over the salmon and avocado and serve.

Strawberry, grapefruit, and yoghurt smoothie

2 servings I Calories: 110
Nutritional values: carbs: 11 gr; protein: 3 gr; fat: 4 gr

Ingredients
✓ 1 pink grapefruit
✓ 1 orange
✓ 1 tsp of grated ginger
✓ 16 strawberries
✓ 200 gr of frozen Greek yoghurt

Directions
➢ Wash and dry the strawberries and then cut them in half.

➢ Put the strawberries in the blender.

- ➢ Peel the grapefruit and orange and cut them into wedges.
- ➢ Put the citrus wedges in the blender.
- ➢ Add the yoghurt and ginger, operate the blender and blend until you get a creamy mixture.
- ➢ Pour the smoothie into two glasses and serve.

Strawberry, yoghurt, and cinnamon smoothie

2 servings I Calories: 100
Nutritional values: carbs: 10 gr; protein: 2 gr; fat: 5 gr

Ingredients
- ✓ 250 gr of strawberries
- ✓ 90 ml of unsweetened almond milk
- ✓ 100 gr of frozen Greek yoghurt
- ✓ 1 tsp of cinnamon powder

Directions
- ➢ Wash the strawberries, dry them, cut them in half and put them in the blender.
- ➢ Add the yoghurt, cinnamon, and almond milk.
- ➢ Operate the blender and blend until you get a creamy and homogeneous mixture.
- ➢ Put the smoothie in two glasses and serve.

Stuffed eggs with salmon

2 servings I Calories: 214
Nutritional values: carbs: 2 gr; protein: 16 gr; fat: 18 gr

Ingredients

- ✓ 4 eggs
- ✓ 150 gr of smoked salmon
- ✓ 100 gr of fresh spreadable cheese
- ✓ Chopped chives to taste
- ✓ Salt and pepper to taste

Directions
- ➢ Put the eggs in a saucepan covered with water. Bring to a boil and cook for another 8 minutes.
- ➢ After cooking, pass the eggs under cold water, shell them and then cut them in half. Remove the yolks and put them in a bowl.
- ➢ Add the salmon cut into small pieces, cheese, salt, pepper, and chives and mix until you get a homogeneous mixture.
- ➢ Put the egg whites on two plates, fill them with the salmon filling and serve.

Turkey rolls

2 servings I Calories 310
Nutritional values: carb 0.2 g, protein 41g, fat 8g

Ingredients:
- ✓ 4 slices of oven roasted turkey breast
- ✓ 2 small cans of tuna, natural
- ✓ 4 tbsp of mayonnaise
- ✓ Oregano to taste

Directions:
- ➢ Combine the tuna with the mayonnaise.
- ➢ Spread the mix onto each turkey breast.
- ➢ Spread the oregano.
- ➢ Roll up the turkey breasts.

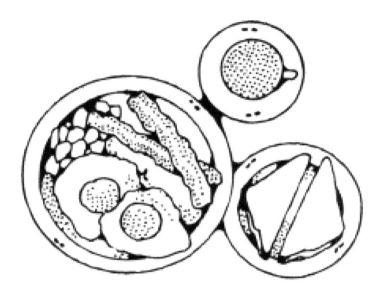

Main courses

Meat recipes

Beef recipes

Beef and leek carpaccio

2 servings I Calories: 370
Nutritional values: carbs: 7 gr; protein: 31 gr; fat: 18 gr

Ingredients
✓ 1 beef fillet of 400 grams
✓ 2 leeks cut into slices
✓ 2 sprigs of parsley
✓ 300 ml of apple cider vinegar
✓ Salt and pepper to taste
✓ Olive oil to taste

Directions
➤ Remove the excess fat from the beef, then wash and dry it. Now cut it into many thin slices.
➤ Clean and cut the leek into slices.
➤ Put the slices of beef and leeks in a baking dish, season with salt and pepper and then cover them with apple cider vinegar.
➤ Cover the pan with aluminium foil and transfer to the fridge to marinate for 3 hours.
➤ After 3 hours, remove the pan from the fridge.
➤ Wash the parsley and then chop it.
➤ Put a drizzle of oil in another pan and brush it to cover the entire surface.
➤ Put a layer of beef on the bottom, put the leeks and parsley on top and season with a little marinade.
➤ Repeat the same operation until all the ingredients are used up.
➤ Once the operation is finished, put the pan on the table and serve.

Cashew and curry marinated beef

2 servings I Calories:420
Nutritional values: carbs: 3 gr; protein: 32 gr; fat: 18 gr

Ingredients
✓ 300 gr of beef fillet
✓ 1 leek
✓ 100 gr of cashews
✓ 1 teaspoon of powdered curry
✓ 20 ml of unsalted soy sauce
✓ 1 leek
✓ 1 garlic clove
✓ Salt and pepper to taste
✓ Olive oil to taste

Directions
➤ First, take the leek, wash it under running water and remove the outer leaves. Cut the end that has the root and the other end with the dark green leaves. After that operation slice it thinly.
➤ Wash and dry the beef fillet, remove the excess fat, and then cut it into cubes.
➤ Peel and wash the garlic and then chop it.

- Put the cashews in a non-stick pan and toast them for 2 minutes.
- Heat 10 ml of olive oil in another pan.
- When oil is hot, put the garlic to brown.
- Add the beef cubes and curry and mix.
- Sauté the beef for a couple of minutes and then add the leek and the unsalted soy sauce.
- Stir, sauté 2/3 minutes and then add half a glass of water.
- Continue cooking for another 8/10 minutes.
- When it's done, you can serve your beef keto dish.

Courgette and spinach beef

2 servings I Calories: 380
Nutritional values: carbs: 8 gr; protein: 34 gr; fat: 12 gr

Ingredients
- ✓ 300 grams of lean beef pulp
- ✓ 1 courgette
- ✓ 1 stick of celery
- ✓ 120 gr of chopped spinach
- ✓ 50 gr of tomato puree
- ✓ A teaspoon of dried thyme
- ✓ Salt and pepper to taste
- ✓ Olive oil to taste

Directions
- First take spinach leaves wash and chop them.
- Remove the celery stalk, the white filaments and then wash it and cut it into small pieces.
- Take the courgette, peel, wash and then cut into cubes.
- Wash and dry the beef meat.

- In a pan, heat a drizzle of olive oil. As soon as it is hot, sauté the spinach for a couple of minutes.
- Now add the celery and mix. Cook for 2 minutes and then add the beef pulp.
- Stir, season with salt and pepper and then add the tomato puree and thyme.
- Add a glass of water, cover with a lid, and cook for 10 minutes.
- Now add the courgettes, add another glass of water, and cook for another 10 minutes.
- Once beef it is ready, place it on serving plates and serve immediately.

Kale and mushroom beef salad

2 servings I Calories: 350
Nutritional values: carbs: 2 gr; protein: 25 gr; fat: 16 gr

Ingredients
- ✓ 300 gr of beef fillet
- ✓ 6 champignon mushrooms
- ✓ 100 grams of kale
- ✓ Apple cider vinegar to taste
- ✓ Salt and pepper to taste
- ✓ Olive oil to taste

Directions
- Wash and dry the beef fillet and season it with salt and pepper.
- Put it in a pan brushed with olive oil and cook in the oven at 200°c for 5/7 minutes.
- Meanwhile, wash and dry the kale.
- Remove the earthy part of the mushrooms, wash them, dry them, and then cut them into thin slices.

As soon as the fillet is cooked, remove it from the oven and let it rest for 5 minutes.

➢ Divide the kale and mushrooms in two serving plates.
➢ Cut the beef fillet into slices and place it on top of the vegetables.
➢ Put one tablespoon of oil, two of apple cider vinegar, salt and pepper in a bowl and mix.
➢ Sprinkle the meat and vegetables with the emulsion and serve.

Parsley and courgettes beef slices

2 servings I Calories: 320
Nutritional values: carbs: 4 gr; protein: 25 gr; fat: 16 gr

Ingredients
✓ 2 slices of beef meat of 150 grams for each
✓ 1 courgette
✓ 1 tbsp of chopped parsley
✓ 100 ml of vegetable (or meat) stock
✓ ½ shallot
✓ Almond flour to taste
✓ Salt and pepper to taste
✓ Olive oil to taste

Directions
➢ First, peel the shallot and then cut it into thin slices.
➢ Peel the courgette, wash it and then cut it into slices too.
➢ Wash and dry the parsley leaves.
➢ Wash and dry the beef slices and then season with salt and pepper.
➢ Put the almond flour on a plate and then flour the slices and set aside.
➢ Heat a tablespoon of oil in a pan and brown the half shallot for a couple of minutes.
➢ Now add the courgettes and sauté

them for a couple of minutes.
➢ Season with salt and pepper, remove the courgettes and put the beef meat.
➢ Brown the meat for 4 minutes per side and then put the courgettes back.
➢ Add the broth and mint and continue cooking for another 4 minutes.
➢ Put the slices and courgettes on serving plates, sprinkle with the cooking juices and serve.

Poultry recipes

Blue cheese bacon and asparagus turkey rolls

2 servings I Calories:430
Nutritional values: carbs: 3 gr; protein: 32 gr; fat: 31 gr

Ingredients
- ✓ 4 slices of turkey breast (100 grams about for each)
- ✓ 150 gr of green asparagus
- ✓ 50 gr of smoked bacon
- ✓ 30 ml of meat stock
- ✓ 20 gr of chopped blue cheese
- ✓ 20 ml of olive oil
- ✓ A sprig of thyme
- ✓ 2 sage leaves
- ✓ Salt and pepper to taste

Directions
- ➢ Start with the asparagus. Remove the hardest parts, peel them sideways then wash and dry them.
- ➢ Put a pot of salted water on the heat. When it comes to a boil, add the asparagus. Let it boil for 5 minutes.
- ➢ After 5 minutes, drain the asparagus and let them cool.
- ➢ Take the turkey slices, wash, and pat them with a paper towel.
- ➢ Place the smoked bacon on each slice of turkey breast first, then the asparagus and finally a little chopped blue cheese.
- ➢ Close the rolls with a toothpick and place them in a pan brushed with a little olive oil.
- ➢ Wash and dry the sage and thyme and place them in the pan with the turkey.
- ➢ Place the rolls in the oven at 220 ° c and set the cooking time to 10/15 minutes.
- ➢ Halfway through cooking, sprinkle the meat with the meat broth and continue cooking.
- ➢ When the turkey is ready, place the meat on two individual plates and sprinkle with the cooking juices.
- ➢ You can serve your keto turkey dish.

Courgette and stilton stuffed chicken

2 servings I Calories: 420
Nutritional values: carbs: 5 gr; protein: 35 gr; fat: 24 gr

Ingredients
- ✓ 2 chicken breast slices (150 grams about for each)
- ✓ 1 courgette
- ✓ 2 sage leaves
- ✓ 2 tbsp of cubed stilton cheese
- ✓ 20 ml of olive oil
- ✓ Salt and pepper to taste.

Directions
- ➢ Start with the courgette.
- ➢ wash it, dry it, and then cut it into thin slices.
- ➢ put a pot with a little salted water, and when it comes to a boil, boil the courgette slices for 3 minutes.
- ➢ Drain and put the courgette to cool.
- ➢ switch to the chicken slices, beating them with a meat mallet to thin them, washing and dry them.
- ➢ Wash and dry the sage too.
- ➢ Meanwhile cut stilton into little cubes.
- ➢ Put the courgette first and then stilton on each slice.

➢ roll the meat on itself and stop the roll with a toothpick.
➢ heat the olive oil in a non-stick pan.
➢ As soon as it is hot, add the sage leaves and then the chicken rolls.
➢ Cook them until the outside of the slices are golden brown and the meat well cooked.
➢ Season with salt and pepper and turn off the heat.
➢ Serve the courgette and stilton stuffed chicken still hot.

Curry chicken and avocado skewers

2 servings I Calories:350
Nutritional values: carbs: 4 gr; protein: 20 gr; fat: 26 gr

Ingredients
✓ 200 grams of chicken breast
✓ 1 ripe avocado
✓ 1 tsp of curry powder
✓ 1 tsp of onion powder
✓ Olive oil to taste
✓ Salt and pepper to taste

Directions
➢ First, remove the excess fat from the chicken breast, then wash it, dry it, and cut it into cubes.
➢ Place the chicken cubes in a bowl and toss with the oil, salt, pepper, onion, and curry powder.
➢ Stir and mix well to flavour the chicken.
➢ Steam the chicken for 10 minutes.
➢ Check the cooking and if it is not cooked yet, continue for another 2/3 minutes.
➢ As soon as it is cooked, place the chicken cubes on a plate.
➢ Peel the avocado, remove the

central stone, and remove the pulp.
➢ Wash the avocado pulp, then cut it into cubes.
➢ Take skewer sticks and form skewers by alternating the avocado cubes with the chicken.
➢ Place the skewers on serving plates with a side of green salad and serve.

Feta and cucumber turkey skewers

2 servings I Calories: 320
Nutritional values: carbs: 4 gr; protein:18 gr; fat: 20 gr

Ingredients
✓ 150 gr of turkey breast
✓ 1 lemon
✓ 1 tsp of powdered ginger
✓ 20 ml of apple cider vinegar
✓ 100 gr of cubed cucumber
✓ 100 gr of cubed feta
✓ 2 cloves of garlic
✓ 10 leaves of parsley
✓ Salt and pepper to taste
✓ Olive oil to taste

Directions

➢ Wash and dry the turkey breast. Remove all excess fat, cut it into cubes and put it in a bowl.
➢ Wash and dry the parsley and then chop it.
➢ Peel and wash the garlic cloves and then chop them.
➢ Put the garlic, parsley, ginger, filtered lemon juice, apple cider vinegar, salt, pepper, and olive oil in the bowl with the meat.

➢ Mix well and then cover the bowl with cling film.
➢ Put the bowl in the fridge and marinate for 2 hours about.
➢ After marinating, remove the bowl from the fridge and start skewered the meat.
➢ Add feta and cucumber cubes and alternate ingredients until they will end.
➢ When all the skewers are ready, reheat a grill and, when it is hot, put the skewers to grill.
➢ Cook for 3 minutes on each side, then remove them from the grill and place them on serving plates.
➢ Sprinkle with the filtered marinating liquid and serve.

Green beans and spinach chicken

2 servings I Calories: 360
Nutritional values: carbs: 4 gr;
protein: 35 gr; fat: 10 gr

Ingredients
✓ 1 whole chicken breast of 400 grams about
✓ 100 gr of green beans
✓ 100 gr of chopped spinach leaves
✓ Half a shallot
✓ Olive oil to taste
✓ Salt and pepper to taste

Directions
➢ Start with the green beans and spinach. Check the green beans, wash them. Wash the spinach leaves as well. And then cook them in boiling salted water for 10 minutes.
➢ Drain and set aside.
➢ Meanwhile, peel and wash the shallot and then chop it.
➢ Wash and dry the chicken, removing all waste.
➢ Take 2 sheets of aluminium foil and brush it with olive oil.
➢ Place the chicken in the centre of every sheet and then add the green beans, the shallot, and the spinach.
➢ Season everything with oil, salt, and pepper and then close the foil and place them in a pan.
➢ Bake in the oven at 200°c for 10/12 minutes about.
➢ As soon as 10 minutes have passed, take the foil out of the oven, let it rest for 5 minutes and then open it carefully.
➢ Place the chicken on a plate with the green beans and spinach garnish, marinating juice and serve.

Ham and cream cheese turkey meatloaf

2 servings I Calories: 410
Nutritional values: carbs: 4 gr;
protein: 32 gr; fat: 22 gr

Ingredients
✓ 250 gr of ground turkey
✓ 2 tbsp of almond flour
✓ 100 gr of sliced ham
✓ 150 gr of cream cheese
✓ 1 tsp of smoked paprika
✓ 1 egg
✓ 60 gr of grated cheddar cheese
✓ 2 sprigs of chopped rosemary
✓ 1 glass of vegetable (or meat) stock
✓ Salt and pepper to taste
✓ Olive oil to taste

Directions
➢ Fist, cut ham into little pieces.

- ➢ In a bowl, mix the minced turkey with the egg, cream cheese, almond flour ham pieces, smoked paprika, a pinch of salt, a pinch of pepper, rosemary, and the cheddar cheese.
- ➢ Work the ingredients until you get a homogeneous mixture.
- ➢ Then roll it out on a sheet of baking paper to obtain a rectangle.
- ➢ Chop the walnuts and sprinkle them on the mixture.
- ➢ Using the paper, roll up the turkey meatloaf and tie the ends with kitchen twine.
- ➢ Prick the paper with a toothpick, transfer the meatloaf into a pan, pour in the broth, add the flaked butter and transfer to the oven.
- ➢ Cook at 210° c for about 15 minutes about.
- ➢ Always check the cooking and, when cooked, remove the turkey meatloaf from the oven.
- ➢ Let it rest for a couple of minutes, then cut the meatloaf into slices, put it on serving plates and serve.

Mushroom and cheddar stuffed chicken

2 servings I Calories: 340
Nutritional values: carbs: 3 gr; protein: 32 gr; fat: 14 gr

Ingredients
- ✓ 400 gr of whole chicken breast 100 gr of button mushrooms
- ✓ 60 gr of grated cheddar cheese
- ✓ 1 garlic clove
- ✓ 1 teaspoon of chopped parsley
- ✓ 2 tbsp of olive oil
- ✓ Salt and pepper to taste

Directions

- ➢ Start with the chicken breast.
- ➢ Wash and dry the chicken meat and then open it in two with a meat knife.
- ➢ Then beat it with a meat mallet to soften it and make it thinner.
- ➢ Remove the earthy part of the button mushrooms, wash them, dry them, and then chop them.
- ➢ Peel and wash the garlic and then put it to brown in a pan with a drizzle of oil.
- ➢ Wash and chop the parsley as well.
- ➢ As soon as it is golden, remove the garlic and brown the button mushrooms for 5 minutes.
- ➢ Season with salt and pepper, add the parsley and turn off the heat.
- ➢ Take the meat and sprinkle it on both sides with salt and pepper.
- ➢ Fill the inside of the meat with the grated cheddar cheese and mushrooms and then roll it up on itself.
- ➢ Seal it well with the help of kitchen twine.
- ➢ Put a drizzle of oil in a pan and brown the roll for 10/15 minutes, turning it on all sides.
- ➢ Once cooked, remove the chicken from the pan and let the meat rest for 5 minutes.
- ➢ Remove the kitchen string and cut the meat into rings.
- ➢ Serve the stuffed chicken sprinkled with the cooking juices.

Pork recipes

Broccoli green pepper and ginger pork loin

2 servings I Calories: 380
Nutritional values: carbs: 5 gr; protein: 31 gr; fat: 22 gr

Ingredients
- ✓ 400 gr of pork loin
- ✓ 200 gr of broccoli tops
- ✓ 20 ml of olive oil
- ✓ 1 tsp of ginger powder
- ✓ 1 tsp of green peppercorns
- ✓ 1 bay leaf
- ✓ ½ lime juice
- ✓ Salt and pepper to taste

Directions
- ➢ Wash and dry the flowers of the broccoli, then cut them into many pieces.
- ➢ Remove any excess fat from the pork tenderloin, then wash and dry it.
- ➢ Wash and dry the bay leaf.
- ➢ Put the olive oil, lime, green peppercorns, salt, ginger powder, and pepper in a bowl and mix with a fork until you get a homogeneous emulsion.
- ➢ Take one sheet of aluminium foil and place the pork loin. Add the broccoli, bay leaf and then wet everything with the oil and lime and green pepper emulsion.
- ➢ Close the foil making sure to seal it well.

- ➢ Put in the oven and cook at 210ºc for 10/12 minutes.
- ➢ When it is ready, remove the bay leaf and serve the pork loin with the broccoli and sprinkled with the marinating liquid.

Curry and coconut pork with green beans

2 servings I Calories: 480
Nutritional values: carbs: 4 gr; protein: 29 gr; fat: 27 gr

Ingredients
- ✓ 400 gr of pork tenderloin
- ✓ 1 clove of garlic
- ✓ 20 gr of fresh grated ginger
- ✓ 200 gr of green beans
- ✓ 200 ml of sugar free coconut milk
- ✓ 10 gr of curry powder
- ✓ 1 lime
- ✓ Salt and pepper to taste
- ✓ Olive oil to taste

Directions
- ➢ Trim the green beans, wash them, and then cut them into two pieces. Steam them for 20 minutes.
- ➢ Meanwhile, wash and dry the pork tenderloin. Remove, if present, bones, and fat and then cut into stripes.
- ➢ Peel and wash the garlic and then chop it.
- ➢ Heat a tablespoon of olive oil in a pan and sauté the garlic clove for a couple of minutes.
- ➢ Now add the pork stripes, stir, and cook for 2/3 minutes.
- ➢ After 3 minutes, add ginger, curry, and a glass of water.
- ➢ Stir and mix everything well and keep on cooking for another 3

minutes.
- ➤ After 3 minutes, add the green beans and coconut milk.
- ➤ Season with salt and pepper, stir and continue for another 5/6 minutes.
- ➤ After this time, turn off and put the chicken on serving plates.
- ➤ Drizzle with the lime juice and serve this keto dish.

Leek and mint sauce pork loin

2 servings I Calories: 320
Nutritional values: carbs: 8 gr; protein: 26 gr; fat: 14 gr

Ingredients
- ✓ 2 slices of pork loin of 150 grams for each
- ✓ 200 ml of meat broth
- ✓ 2 leeks
- ✓ Salt and pepper to taste
- ✓ Olive oil to taste
- ✓ 2 mint leaves
- ✓ 2 sprigs of rosemary

Directions
- ➤ Wash and dry the pork loin.
- ➤ Wash and dry the mint and rosemary.
- ➤ Remove the stalk and the hard outer leaves, then wash them and cut them into rings.
- ➤ Take a pan and heat some oil. Brown the fillet for two minutes on each side, season with salt and pepper and then remove it.
- ➤ Now add the aromatic herbs and then the leeks.
- ➤ Sauté everything for 3 minutes, season with salt and pepper and then add the meat broth.

- ➤ Cook for 7 minutes over medium heat.
- ➤ When 7 minutes have passed, add the pork loin, and cook for another 3/4 minutes, turning the meat only once.
- ➤ Take the plates, put the pork, sprinkle with the leek sauce, and serve.

Pork fillet with cheddar

2 servings I Calories: 390
Nutritional values: carbs: 6 gr; protein: 22 gr; fat: 2 gr

Ingredients
- ✓ 2 pork fillets of 150 grams for each
- ✓ 120 gr of chopped cheddar
- ✓ 1 pinch of onion powder
- ✓ Dried oregano to taste
- ✓ Olive oil to taste
- ✓ Salt and pepper to taste.
Directions
- ➤ Wash and dry the pork tenderloin.
- ➤ Brush a pan with olive oil, lay the meat on the bottom and then sprinkle the chopped cheddar with olive oil.
- ➤ Season with oil, salt and pepper and then put the onion powder and dried oregano on top.
- ➤ Cook at 210 ° for 10/15 minutes.
- ➤ Once cooked, remove the pan from the oven, let the meat rest for 5 minutes and then serve the meat sprinkled with the cooking juices and the melted cheese.

Spinach and pine nuts roasted pork

2 servings I Calories: 360
Nutritional values: carbs: 4 gr; protein:
26 gr; fat: 18 gr

Ingredients
- ✓ 2 slices of pork tenderloin of 150 grams for each
- ✓ 300 gr of spinach
- ✓ Half shallot
- ✓ 20 gr of chopped pine nuts
- ✓ Salt and pepper to taste
- ✓ Olive oil to taste

Directions
- ➤ First, wash and pat the pork loin with a paper towel and then cut it into strips.
- ➤ Peel and wash the shallot and then chop it.
- ➤ Wash and dry the spinach and then chop it.
- ➤ Put a tablespoon of olive oil in a pan and then add the shallot.
- ➤ Brown it for a couple of minutes and then add the pork tenderloin.
- ➤ Sauté for 2 minutes, season with salt and pepper and then remove and set aside.
- ➤ Now put the spinach in the same pan.
- ➤ Cook for 5 minutes, then season with salt and pepper.
- ➤ Now take the pork loin and return it to the pan with the spinach. Continue cooking for another 2/3 minutes.
- ➤ Meanwhile, toast and chop the pine nuts.
- ➤ Once the pork loin has finished cooking, turn it off and distribute it on plates, along with the spinach.
- ➤ Sprinkle the meat with the chopped pine nuts and serve.

Fish recipes

Courgettes and pink pepper tuna

2 servings I Calories: 410
Nutritional values: carbs: 7 gr; protein: 30 gr; fat: 25 gr

Ingredients
- ✓ 300 gr of tuna fillets
- ✓ 2 medium sized courgettes
- ✓ ½ chopped shallot
- ✓ 1 tsp of chopped dill
- ✓ Olive oil to taste
- ✓ Salt to taste
- ✓ 1 tbsp of pink pepper

Directions
- ➢ First, you can peel the courgettes, wash them, dry them, and then cut them into slices.
- ➢ Put courgettes into a baking pan.
- ➢ Wash and dry dill and then place in the pan with courgettes. Add one teaspoon of olive oil, chopped shallot salt and mix.
- ➢ Transfer the pan into preheated oven (210° c).
- ➢ Let cook for 5 minutes about, or until they are well cooked.
- ➢ Meanwhile, wash and dry the tuna filets.
- ➢ Remove the baking pan from the oven and add the tuna fillet

and the pink pepper.
- ➢ Cook for another 10 minutes about.
- ➢ When fish and courgettes will be cooked remove from the oven.
- ➢ Let it rest for a couple of minutes and then cut the tuna into slices.
- ➢ Place the courgettes on the bottom of the plate and the tuna fillets on top and serve.

Fennel curry plaice

2 servings I Calories: 350
Nutritional values: carbs: 3 gr protein: 30 gr; fat: 12 gr

Ingredients
- ✓ 2 plaice fillet (150 grams about for each)
- ✓ 120 gr of fennels
- ✓ ½ tsp of curry powder
- ✓ 1 pinch of smoked paprika
- ✓ ½ lime
- ✓ 1 tbsp olive oil
- ✓ Salt and pepper to taste

Directions
- ➢ Start the recipe with clearing the fennels.
- ➢ Eliminate the inner part, separate the various leaves, wash them under running water, dry them and then cut the fennel into thin slices.
- ➢ Wash some pieces of remaining fennel as well and set them aside.
- ➢ Take a pan and heat a bit of olive oil.
- ➢ When oil will be hot the fennel slices for about 5/6 minutes to sauté, adding salt and a drop of water.
- ➢ Now switch to the plaice fillet.
- ➢ Wash them under running water and check that there are no bones.

Now take a pan and put 3 sheets of parchment paper inside the pan.
- ➢ Grease the parchment paper with a little oil, add the plaice, salt it, sprinkle it with curry and paprika.
- ➢ Then sprinkle plaice with the lime juice and a drizzle of olive oil and the fennel pieces that you had set aside.
- ➢ Put the plaice in a preheated oven at 210° f for about 8/10 minutes about.
- ➢ Once plaice fillets are ready, remove from the parchment paper.
- ➢ Also remove the fennel pieces too and place plaice in a serving dish surrounded by previously cooked fennel.
- ➢ Serve this keto dish still hot.

Ginger trout with asparagus

2 servings I Calories: 380
Nutritional values: carbs: 1 gr; protein: 22 gr; fat: 24 gr

Ingredients
- ✓ 400 gr of trout fillets
- ✓ 200 gr of fresh asparagus
- ✓ 30 ml of olive oil
- ✓ 1 pinch of paprika
- ✓ 1 pinch of salt
- ✓ Pepper as needed
- ✓ 1 sprig of parsley
- ✓ 10 grams of powdered ginger

Directions
- ➢ First wash the asparagus well, eliminating the white part of the stem and keeping the more tender tips aside.
- ➢ Meanwhile, take the trout fillets and rinse them under running water.
- ➢ Dry them well with a kitchen paper towel.

- ➢ Sprinkle the trout fillets with salt and pepper in both sides.
- ➢ Sprinkle over the ginger and paprika as well.
- ➢ Lightly oil a baking sheet and place the asparagus first and then the trout fillets.
- ➢ Bake in a preheated oven at 210°c for about 10 minutes about.
- ➢ Check both the doneness of the fish and the asparagus.
- ➢ As soon as they are ready, serve the trout fillets hot on the asparagus bed.
- ➢ Sprinkle everything with parsley and serve your keto dish.

Haddock meatballs

2 servings I Calories: 230
Nutritional values: carbs: 5 gr; protein: 16 gr; fat: 18 gr

Ingredients
- ✓ 200 grams of haddock fillet
- ✓ 2 tablespoons of almond flour
- ✓ 2 tablespoons of unsweetened vegetable milk
- ✓ Olive oil to taste
- ✓ Salt, pepper to taste

To bread:
- ✓ An egg
- ✓ Almond flour to taste

Directions
- ➢ First, clean the haddock thoroughly by removing the skin and bone.
- ➢ Put it in a non-stick pan with a drizzle of oil and cook over medium heat.
- ➢ While the haddock is cooking, put the almond flour in a bowl and pour in the vegetable milk, stirring.
- ➢ Once the fish is ready, put it in a blender with the almond flour and

milk, add salt and pepper and blend until smooth.

➤ Prepare the ingredients for the breading by placing them in three bowls.

➤ With the help of a teaspoon take a quantity of mixture and with your hands create some meatballs.

➤ Pass them first in the almond flour, then in the egg and finally in the almond flour again.

➤ Cook the meatballs in the oven at 200°c for about 5/6 minutes.

➤ When the haddock balls are golden brown, remove them from the oven

➤ Add salt and serve hot.

Leeks and tuna croquettes

2 servings I Calories: 270
Nutritional values: carbs: 6 gr; protein: 18 gr; fat: 19 gr

Ingredients
✓ 200 gr of cooked leeks
✓ 200 gr of cooked tuna fillet
✓ 2 tbsp of almond flour
✓ 150 ml of cooking cream
✓ 2 tbsp of grated parmesan cheese
✓ 1 tbsp of mixed aromatic herbs (parsley, thyme, basil, rosemary)
✓ Olive oil to taste
✓ Salt and pepper to taste

Directions
➤ First, you should cut cooked tuna into pieced.

➤ Now, pass both leeks and tuna through a vegetable mill until they are creamy and collect the mixture in a bowl.

➤ In another bowl, put the cooking cream, the almond flour and add the parmesan cheese, the chopped aromatic herbs, salt, and pepper.

➤ Mix carefully and add this mixture to the cream of leeks and tuna, mixing again carefully.

➤ Let the dough rest for a few minutes, then form a sort of oval croquettes with them, which you will pass repeatedly into other almond flour.

➤ Smoke abundant olive oil in the frying pan and dip in a few tuna and leeks croquettes at a time, making them well browned on each side. As they are ready, place them on a sheet of absorbent kitchen paper and keep them warm.

➤ Serve this keto tuna and leeks croquettes still hot.

Lemon and herbs haddock

2 servings I Calories: 360
Nutritional values: carbs: 2 gr; protein: 30 gr; fat: 22 gr

Ingredients
✓ 2 haddock filets of 160 grams about for each
✓ 120 ml of fresh and sugar free lemon juice
✓ 1 tbsp of dry thyme
✓ 1 tbsp of chopped coriander
✓ 1tsp of dry oregano
✓ 1 tsp of ground cinnamon
✓ 20 ml of olive oil
✓ Salt and pepper to taste

Directions
➤ Let's start by cleaning the haddock fillets.

➤ Wash them under running water, remove the skin and if there are bones with fish tweezers.

➢ Rinse the haddock quickly under running water and then dry it with paper towel.
➢ Sprinkle the haddock fillets with a little salt and pepper and set aside.
➢ In a small bowl, put together the fresh lemon juice, a tablespoon of olive oil, cinnamon and dried oregano, a pinch of salt and pepper.
➢ Combine well everything.
➢ Wash both thyme and coriander, then chop very coarsely.
➢ Take a pan large.
➢ Put the haddock in the pan and brush it with a little olive oil.
➢ Sprinkle both thyme and coriander the on top.
➢ Put the pan to bake in a preheated oven at 210ºc for 10 minutes about.
➢ Check the cooking and, if necessary, continue cooking for another 2/3 minutes.
➢ Serve the haddock with all the herbs and cooking juice.

Lime and mint marinated cod with green olives

2 servings I Calories: 305
Nutritional values: carbs: 4 gr; protein: 28 gr; fat: 10 gr

Ingredients
✓ 2 cod of about 200 grams for each
✓ 10 green olives, pitted
✓ 30 ml of olive oil
✓ Half a glass of lime juice
✓ A lime cut into slices
✓ 4 mint leaves
✓ Salt and pepper to taste

Directions
1. Gently clean and gut and wash the cod fillets, without removing the head.
2. Let them drain well.
3. Then gently dry them with a cloth and put a pinch of salt and pepper and the well washed mint leaves in the abdomen.
4. Pour a little oil into a baking pan.
5. Arrange the cod, sprinkle with lime juice and sprinkle with a little salt.
6. Place the dish in a hot oven at 210 ° c, leaving the cod to cook for about 10/15 minutes.
7. Sprinkle it from time to time with the cooking juices, until the skin is golden and crisp.
8. Halfway through cooking, add the green olives (10 minutes).
9. Bring to the table in the same pan with lime slices.

Mackerel in foil

2 servings I Calories: 370
Nutritional values: carbs: 4 gr; protein: 29 gr; fat: 20 gr

Ingredients
✓ 2 mackerel fillets of 150 grams for each
✓ 2 tbsp of chopped shallot
✓ Two bay leaves
✓ A bunch of parsley
✓ 2 anchovy fillets
✓ 4 tablespoons of olive oil
✓ A tablespoon of apple cider vinegar
✓ The juice of half a lime
✓ Salt and pepper to taste

Directions
➢ Clean, gut and wash the mackerel, then dry them, keep them whole, including the head.
➢ Make a slight incision on the sides to facilitate cooking.
➢ Wash and chop both the shallot and

parsley.

➢ Prepare the sauce with the clean chopped anchovy fillets sprinkled with the apple cider vinegar, lime juice, shallot, and finely chopped parsley, a pinch of salt and pepper and two tablespoons of olive oil.

➢ Cut out a heart-shaped aluminium foil, so that it can contain the fish and lightly butter it.

➢ Arrange the mackerel, sprinkle with the sauce and whole bay leaves.

➢ Lightly grease the surface with the remaining oil and form a foil, carefully folding the edges, but keeping the aluminium foil detached from the sides of the fish, so that during cooking there is room for the steam that will form.

➢ Place the bag on the basket of the oven heated to 210 ° c for 10/12 minutes.

➢ Serve the keto mackerel in foil on a serving plate, but still wrapped in the foil.

Pecans and parmesan crusted salmon

2 servings I Calories: 420
Nutritional values: carbs: 3 gr; protein: 32 gr; fat: 30 gr

Ingredients
✓ 2 salmon fillets of (about 200 grams for each)
✓ 2 rosemary leaves
✓ 20 gr of chopped pecans
✓ 20 gr of grated parmesan cheese
✓ 2 tbsp of olive oil
✓ Salt and pepper to taste

Directions

➢ First, start with cleaning both salmon fillet.

➢ Remove the skin and any bone, and then wash it very well.

➢ Dry the salmon fillets with a kitchen paper towel.

➢ At this point you can cut salmon fillets into small slices.

➢ Now sprinkle them on both sides with salt and pepper.

➢ Wash and dry rosemary sprigs.

➢ Place 2 slices of salmon on a cutting board, place 1 rosemary leaf inside.

➢ Close the salmon slices, sealing them with toothpicks.

➢ Mix the chopped pecans with the grated parmesan cheese.

➢ Pass the slices over the pecans and parmesan cheese, pressing them to make the breading adhere well.

➢ Heat the olive oil in a pan and as soon as it is hot, put the breaded salmon to brown.

➢ Turn them over and cook until the salmon is well cooked and golden on the outside.

➢ Serve the pecans crusted salmon immediately and hot, sprinkled with its cooking juices.

Mushrooms and bay haddock

2 servings I Calories: 390
Nutritional values: carbs: 4 gr; protein: 34 gr; fat: 20 gr

Ingredients
✓ 2 haddock fillet (150 grams about for each)
✓ 150 gr of button mushrooms
✓ 1 garlic clove
✓ ½ lemon

✓ 2 bay leaves
✓ Salt and pepper to taste

Directions
➢ First, preheat the oven to 210°c.
➢ Clean the haddock fillets under running water and dry them.
➢ Proceed, in the meantime, cleaning the mushrooms too with a cloth, removing any soil.
➢ Cut the button mushrooms into little pieces.
➢ Peel and chop the garlic clove as well.
➢ Spread some baking paper on a baking sheet and place garlic and button mushrooms pieces in the centre of the pan.
➢ Place the haddock fillet on the side.
➢ Season haddock with salt and pepper.
➢ Squeeze the lemon over it.
➢ Add th e washed and chopped bay leaves.
➢ Close the parchment paper and cook the haddock in a preheated oven for about 10/12 minutes.
➢ Always check the cooking of the haddock and mushrooms.
➢ You can serve when the haddock and mushrooms are cooked.
➢ Serve this keto main course still hot.

Pistachio and chilli haddock

2 servings I Calories:400
Nutritional values: carbs: 6 gr; protein: 23 gr; fat: 22 gr

Ingredients
✓ 2 haddock fillets of 150 grams about
✓ 20 gr of chopped pistachios
✓ 20 gr of olive oil
✓ 1 tsp of chilli powder
✓ Salt and pepper to taste

Directions
➢ First, clean the haddock fillets from any bones, rinse and dry them with a paper towel.
➢ Cut haddock lengthwise to obtain slices.
➢ Try not to cut too thick fish slices.
➢ Put the haddock slices in a baking pan and sprinkle them with the olive oil.
➢ Season haddock with chilli powder, salt, and pepper.
➢ Take the slices of haddock and pass them in the pistachio breading making sure to press well so that it is breaded on all sides.
➢ Put a tablespoon of olive oil in a non-stick pan and let it heat up.
➢ As soon as the oil starts to sizzle, place the breaded haddock slices in the pan and cook them for a couple of minutes on both sides.
➢ Cook until the haddock will be soft.
➢ As soon as the breaded pistachios slices of haddock are cooked, place them on a serving dish and serve.

Place in caper tabasco butter

2 servings I Calories: 395
Nutritional values: carbs: 6 gr; protein: 28 gr; fat: 29 gr

Ingredients
✓ 300 gr of already cleaned plaice fillet
✓ 60 gr of butter
✓ 1 tsp of tabasco sauce
✓ 20 gr of chopped capers
✓ Olive oil to taste
✓ Salt and pepper to taste

Directions

➢ Wash and dry the plaice fillet.
➢ Rinse the capers and then squeeze and chop them.
➢ Now heat a bit of olive oil in a pan.
➢ When it is hot enough, put the plaice to cook.
➢ Cook for 4 minutes per side, season with salt and pepper and turn off.
➢ While the plaice is cooking, put the butter in a saucepan.
➢ Melt the butter completely and then add the capers and tabasco sauce.
➢ Cook for a couple of minutes and then turn off.
➢ Once the plaice is cooked, remove it from the pan and place it on the plate.
➢ Sprinkle the plaice with the caper and tabasco butter and serve.

Salmon in cranberry sauce

2 servings I Calories: 490
Nutritional values: carbs: 6 gr; protein: 36 gr; fat: 32 gr

Ingredients
✓ 2 salmon fillets of 200 grams for each
✓ 100 gr of fresh cranberry juice (no added sugar)
✓ 1 lime
✓ 10 gr of fresh grated ginger
✓ 20 ml of unsalted soy sauce
✓ Olive oil to taste
✓ Salt and pepper to taste

Directions
➢ Start with the sauce. In a bowl, mix the filtered fresh cranberry juice, ginger, soy sauce, filtered lime juice, salt, pepper and 10 ml of olive oil.
➢ Remove any bones and skin from the salmon fillets, wash the and

place in the bowl with the cranberry sauce.
➢ Put to marinate in the fridge for 50/60 minutes.
➢ After this marinating time, take a pan and place the salmon inside.
➢ Sprinkle the salmon fillets with the cranberry sauce and then let cook in the oven preheated at 200 ° c for 10/12 minutes.
➢ Once the salmon is well cooked, remove the pan from the oven.
➢ Place the salmon fillets on serving plates and serve immediately sprinkled with the remaining cranberry sauce

Strawberry and smoked salmon salad

2 servings I Calories: 170
Nutritional values: carbs: 6 gr; protein: 13 gr; fat: 14 gr

Ingredients
✓ 80 gr of strawberries
✓ 100 gr of smoked salmon
✓ 1 tbsp of chia seeds
✓ Apple cider vinegar to taste
✓ Salt and pepper to taste
✓ Olive oil to taste

Directions
➢ First, wash and dry the strawberries and then cut them into slices.
➢ Cut the smoked salmon into slices too.
➢ Put the strawberries and salmon in a salad bowl.
➢ In a small bowl, emulsify the apple cider vinegar, oil, salt, and pepper together.
➢ Sprinkle the salad with the emulsion and chia seeds. Mix gently.

➢ You can serve your keto salad.

Tuna and cheddar meatballs

2 servings I Calories: 240
Nutritional values: carbs: 2 gr; protein:
20 gr; fat: 21 gr

Ingredients
✓ 200 gr of tuna in oil
✓ 1 egg
✓ 100 grams of grated cheddar
cheese
✓ 60 gr of almond flour
✓ 1 tsp of chopped mint

Directions
➢ First, you can open and drain the
cans of tuna.
➢ Put the tuna in a bowl and mash
with a fork.
➢ Add the egg, cheddar, finely
chopped mint and almond flour.
➢ Form some meatballs and let them
rest for some minute.
➢ Take a baking tray and cover it with
parchment paper.
➢ Wet the bottom with a bit olive oil
and place the tuna and cheddar
meatballs on top.
➢ Cook, turning them halfway through
cooking, for about 8/10 minutes at
210°c, or until they are golden
brown.
➢ Allow to cool slightly and serve this
keto tuna and cheddar meatballs.

Vegetable recipes

Cheddar and pecans asparagus

2 servings I Calories: 170
Nutritional values: carbs: 3 gr; protein: 10 gr; fat: 14 gr

Ingredients
- ✓ 250 gr of green asparagus
- ✓ 20 gr of chopped pecans
- ✓ 1 sprig of thyme
- ✓ 30 gr of grated cheddar cheese
- ✓ Salt and pepper to taste
- ✓ Butter to taste

Directions
- ➢ First, eliminate the final and harder part of the green asparagus, then wash them and let them drain.
- ➢ Bring a pot of water and salt to a boil and then put the asparagus to boil for 5/6 minutes.
- ➢ Once cooked, drain, and let the asparagus cool.
- ➢ Brush a baking pan with butter and then put the green asparagus inside.
- ➢ Sprinkle with cheddar, pecans and thyme and then put the baking pan in the oven.
- ➢ Cook at 200°c f for 5/6 minutes.
- ➢ Once cooked, remove the cheesy asparagus from the oven, put them on the plate and serve still hot.

Courgette and thyme cream

2 servings I Calories: 70
Nutritional values: carbs: 2 gr; protein: 8 gr; fat: 3 gr

Ingredients
- ✓ 2 small courgettes
- ✓ 20 gr of chopped thyme
- ✓ 1 tsp of onion powder
- ✓ 1 teaspoon of turmeric
- ✓ Olive oil to taste
- ✓ 400 ml of water
- ✓ Salt and pepper to taste

Directions
- ➢ Start with peeling the courgettes. After this operation, wash them and then cut them into small pieces.
- ➢ Put a tablespoon of olive oil in a saucepan and let it heat up.
- ➢ Add the courgettes, onion powder and turmeric and brown for 5 minutes.
- ➢ Add the washed and chopped thyme, salt and pepper and mix.
- ➢ Now add 400 ml of water and keep on cooking for another 10 minutes.
- ➢ After 10 minutes, turn off and blend everything with an immersion blender, until you get a smooth and homogeneous mixture.
- ➢ Put the courgette and thyme cream on plates, season with a drizzle of oil and serve.

Garlic creamy courgette

2 servings I Calories: 160
Nutritional values: carbs: 6 gr; protein: 10 gr; fat: 12 gr

Ingredients
- ✓ 2 medium courgettes
- ✓ 150 gr of Greek yoghurt

- ✓ 10 gr of garlic powder 2 tbsp of dried buttermilk
- ✓ 1 tbsp of chopped herb mix
- ✓ Olive oil to taste

Directions
- ➤ First, peel the courgettes.
- ➤ Wash them, dry, and then cut them into pieces.
- ➤ Brush the courgette pieces with the Greek yoghurt.
- ➤ Combine the herbs and garlic powder in a bowl.
- ➤ Place the courgettes on a baking pan.
- ➤ Dust the courgettes with the garlic and herbs mixture.
- ➤ Cook in the hot oven at 205° c for 10/12 minutes.
- ➤ Serve creamy courgettes still hot.

Grilled orange kale

2 servings I Calories: 55
Nutritional values: carbs: 1 gr; protein: 6 gr; fat: 3 gr

Ingredients for 4 servings
- ✓ 400 gr of kale
- ✓ Juice of half orange
- ✓ 1 pinch of chilli powder
- ✓ Olive oil to taste
- ✓ Salt and pepper to taste

Directions
- ➤ First, take the bunches of kale, remove the outer leaves, equalize the cores, and clean them well.
- ➤ Wash kale leaves under running water and put them to dry on a cloth.
- ➤ Now, place them on a plate and season with a little oil.
- 1. Heat up a grill with a bit of olive oil.

- ➤ Put the bunches of kale in it and grill them first on one side then on the other, five minutes of cooking will be enough.
- ➤ Then, put kale leaves in a serving dish and season with salt, pepper, chilli powder and orange juice, if you want you can now add a little oil.
- ➤ You can serve this keto dish.

Parmesan and green bean salad

2 servings I Calories: 240
Nutritional values: carbs: 2 gr; protein: 14 gr; fat: 19 gr

Ingredients
- ✓ 250 gr of boiled green beans
- ✓ 120 gr of cubed parmesan cheese
- ✓ ½ shallot
- ✓ 2 tsp of chia seeds
- ✓ Salt and pepper to taste
- ✓ Olive oil to taste

Directions
- ➤ First, put the boiled green beans divided into 2 serving dishes.
- ➤ Place the washed and chopped half shallot, parmesan cubes and chia seeds on top of every dish.
- ➤ Season with oil, salt, and pepper.
- ➤ You can serve this very easy salad.

Spinach and cheddar gratin

2 servings I Calories: 280
Nutritional values: carbs: 2 gr; protein: 16 gr; fat: 22 gr

Ingredients
- ✓ 300 gr of spinach leaves
- ✓ 100 ml of no sugar almond milk
- ✓ 100 ml of sour cream

- ✓ 1 pinch of nutmeg
- ✓ 100 gr of grated cheddar cheese
- ✓ Salt and pepper to taste

Directions
- ➤ First, preheat the oven at 200°c.
- ➤ Meanwhile, wash, and chop spinach leaves.
- ➤ In a bowl, mix the almond milk and sour cream and season to taste with salt, pepper, and nutmeg.
- ➤ Coat the spinach with the almond milk mixture.
- ➤ Transfer the spinach in a baking pan.
- ➤ Place the baking pan in the oven.
- ➤ Set the timer to 7 minutes and bake the gratin.
- ➤ After 5 minutes pour over cheddar cheese.
- ➤ Set the timer again for 5 minutes again and bake the spinach and cheddar gratin until it is browned.
- ➤ Serve spinach gratin still hot.

Stilton cucumber and egg salad

2 servings I Calories: 390
Nutritional values: carbs: 2 gr; protein: 20 gr; fat: 22 gr

Ingredients
- ✓ 200 gr of cubed stilton cheese
- ✓ 2 eggs
- ✓ 1 cucumber
- ✓ 1 small lime
- ✓ Apple cider vinegar to taste
- ✓ Olive oil to taste
- ✓ Salt and pepper to taste

Directions
- ➤ First cook the eggs.
- ➤ Place the eggs directly in a full

water saucepan and let them harden for about 8 minutes from boiling.
- ➤ Once they will be cooked, let them cool, then peel them and cut them into wedges.
- ➤ Now you can move on to the other ingredients.
- ➤ Clean the cucumber and slice it.
- ➤ Cube stilton cheese.
- ➤ In a small bowl combine the lime juice with a bit of apple cider vinegar and the oil.
- ➤ Emulsify well, adding a pinch of salt as well.
- ➤ Arrange a bed of cucumber in the individual serving dishes, then add the eggs and stilton cheese.
- ➤ Sprinkle with the vinegar emulsion and serve.

Tofu and avocado tartar

2 servings I Calories: 210
Nutritional values: carbs: 4 gr; protein: 14 gr; fat: 18 gr

Ingredients
- ✓ 120 gr of cubed tofu
- ✓ 1 ripe avocado
- ✓ 1 tablespoon of soy sauce
- ✓ 1 lime
- ✓ 1 tsp of flax seeds
- ✓ 1 tsp of chopped chives
- ✓ Salt and pepper to taste
- ✓ Olive oil to taste

Directions
- ➤ First, rinse quickly and then dab the tofu with a paper towel, then cube.
- ➤ Season tofu with oil, salt, pepper, the juice of half a lime and the soy sauce.

- ➢ Peel the avocado, remove the stone, and then cut the pulp into cubes.
- ➢ Put the cubed avocado in another bowl and season with the juice of half a lime, oil, salt, and pepper.
- ➢ Take two dishes and distribute the avocado on the bottom. Then put the tofu cubes on top.
- ➢ Decorate the surface with flat seeds and chopped chives and serve.

Salads

Avocado, chicken, and pink grapefruit salad

2 servings I Calories: 415
Nutritional values: carbs: 10 gr; protein: 26 gr; fat: 10 gr

Ingredients
- ✓ 200 gr of chicken breast
- ✓ ½ lemon
- ✓ 1 avocado
- ✓ 1 tbsp of apple cider vinegar
- ✓ 1 pink grapefruit
- ✓ 100 gr of valerian
- ✓ Salt and pepper to taste
- ✓ Olive oil to taste

Directions
- ➢ Remove the fat from the chicken and then cut it into thin slices.
- ➢ Heat some oil in a pan and cook the chicken for 10 minutes, turning it often. After 10 minutes, season with salt and pepper and turn off.
- ➢ Peel the avocado, remove the stone, and then cut the pulp into slices.
- ➢ Wash and dry the valerian.
- ➢ Peel the grapefruit and cut the pulp into cubes.
- ➢ Put the valerian, avocado, grapefruit, and chicken in a bowl.
- ➢ Season with vinegar, salt, pepper, oil, and lemon juice.
- ➢ Mix the salad well and serve.

Egg, salmon, and tomato salad

2 servings I Calories: 212
Nutritional values: carbs: 3 gr; protein: 13 gr; fat: 12 gr

Ingredients
- ✓ 100 gr of smoked salmon
- ✓ 50 gr of cherry tomatoes
- ✓ 2 eggs
- ✓ 100 gr of lettuce
- ✓ ½ lemon
- ✓ Pink peppercorns to taste
- ✓ Salt and pepper to taste
- ✓ Olive oil to taste

Directions
- ➢ Put the eggs in a saucepan, cover them with cold water and bring to a boil. Continue cooking for another 8 minutes, then pass them under cold water, shell them and cut them into wedges.
- ➢ Wash the lettuce, dry it, and then cut it into small pieces.
- ➢ Wash the cherry tomatoes and cut them in half.
- ➢ Put the cherry tomatoes, lettuce, and eggs in a bowl.
- ➢ Cut the salmon into small pieces and put it in the bowl with the other ingredients.
- ➢ Squeeze the lemon into a bowl and add salt, pepper and oil and mix well.
- ➢ Pour the emulsion over the salad, mix gently, and serve.

Grapefruit, rocket, and raspberry salad

2 servings I Calories: 260

Nutritional values: carb: 8 gr; protein: 6 gr; fat: 12 gr

Ingredients
- ✓ 1 pink grapefruit
- ✓ 100 gr of rocket salad
- ✓ 100 gr of feta cheese
- ✓ 8 raspberries
- ✓ Olive oil to taste
- ✓ Salt and pepper to taste

Directions
- ➢ Wash and dry the rocket salad and place it in a bowl.
- ➢ Peel the grapefruit, remove the white part, and cut the pulp into cubes.
- ➢ Wash and dry the raspberries.
- ➢ Cut the feta into cubes.
- ➢ Put the feta cheese, grapefruit pulp and raspberries in the bowl with the rocket.
- ➢ Season with oil, salt, and pepper, mix well and serve.

Green bean and feta salad

2 servings I Calories: 250
Nutritional values: carb: 9 gr; protein: 7 gr; fat: 10 gr

Ingredients
- ✓ 250 gr of green beans
- ✓ 50 gr of Greek feta
- ✓ 25 gr of toasted walnut kernels
- ✓ 5 cherry tomatoes
- ✓ 4 basil leaves
- ✓ Olive oil to taste
- ✓ Salt and pepper to taste

Directions
- ➢ Chop the green beans and wash them under running water.
- ➢ Put the green beans to cook in salted boiling water for 10 minutes.

- ➢ After 10 minutes, drain the green beans and pass them under cold water.
- ➢ Wash the cherry tomatoes and leave them whole.
- ➢ Put the green beans, cherry tomatoes, and diced feta in a bowl.
- ➢ Add the walnut kernels and the washed and chopped basil leaves.
- ➢ Season with oil, salt, and pepper, mix well and serve.

Mozzarella, bacon, and blueberry salad

2 servings I Calories: 296
Nutritional values: carbs: 6 gr; protein: 12 gr; fat: 26 gr

Ingredients
- ✓ 125 gr of rocket salad
- ✓ 1 mozzarella
- ✓ 40 gr of walnut kernels
- ✓ 50 gr of blueberries
- ✓ 4 slices of bacon
- ✓ Olive oil to taste
- ✓ Salt and pepper to taste

Directions
- ➢ Wash and dry the rocket salad and place it in a bowl.
- ➢ Wash the blueberries and place them in the bowl with the rocket salad.
- ➢ Cut the mozzarella into cubes and put it with the rest of the ingredients.
- ➢ Roll the bacon slices on themselves and place them in the bowl.
- ➢ Add the walnuts, season with oil, salt, and pepper.
- ➢ Mix well and serve.

Pumpkin salad with mushrooms and almonds

2 servings I Calories: 270
Nutritional values: carb: 10 gr; protein: 3 gr; fat: 6 gr

Ingredients
- ✓ 250 gr of pumpkin pulp
- ✓ 150 gr of champignon mushrooms
- ✓ 1 tbsp of sliced almonds
- ✓ 100 gr of green salad
- ✓ 1 sprig of rosemary
- ✓ Salt and pepper to taste
- ✓ Olive oil to taste

Directions
- ➢ Wash the pumpkin pulp and cut it into thin slices.
- ➢ Wash and dry the mushrooms and then cut them into slices.
- ➢ Brush a baking pan with olive oil and put the pumpkin and mushrooms inside.
- ➢ Season with oil, salt, and pepper, add the rosemary and put the baking pan in the oven.
- ➢ Cook at 200 ° c for 15 minutes.
- ➢ After cooking, remove the baking pan from the oven and put the pumpkin and mushrooms on two plates.
- ➢ Add the green salad, washed and dried, season with oil, salt and pepper and serve.

Salad with bacon, tomatoes, and eggs

2 servings I Calories: 288
Nutritional values: carbs: 6 gr; protein: 11 gr; fat: 21 gr

Ingredients
- ✓ 200 gr of green salad
- ✓ 80 gr of sliced bacon
- ✓ 3 eggs
- ✓ 2 ripe red tomatoes
- ✓ ½ onion
- ✓ Apple cider vinegar to taste
- ✓ Salt and pepper to taste
- ✓ Olive oil to taste

Directions
- ➢ Put the eggs in a saucepan, cover them with cold water and bring to a boil. Continue cooking for another 8 minutes, then pass them under cold water, shell them and cut them into wedges.
- ➢ Wash and dry the green salad and place it in a bowl.
- ➢ Wash the tomatoes and cut them into cubes.
- ➢ Peel the onion and cut it into slices.
- ➢ Put the tomatoes and the onion in the bowl with the green salad.
- ➢ Cut the bacon into strips and put it in the bowl with the other ingredients.
- ➢ Season with apple cider vinegar, salt, pepper, and olive oil. Mix the salad well and serve.

Salmon, tomato, and lemon salad

2 servings I Calories: 160
Nutritional values: carbs: 4 gr; protein: 22 gr; fat: 8 gr

Ingredients
- ✓ 200 gr of salmon
- ✓ 5 cherry tomatoes
- ✓ 4 lettuce leaves
- ✓ 1 lemon
- ✓ Chopped chives to taste

✓ Olive oil to taste
✓ Salt and pepper to taste

Directions
➢ Wash the salmon, dry it, remove the skin and bones, and then cut it into cubes.
➢ Put the salmon in a pan with hot olive oil and cook for 5 minutes. Season with salt and pepper and then turn off.
➢ Wash and dry the lettuce leaves and cut them into pieces.
➢ Wash the cherry tomatoes and cut them in half.
➢ Put the lettuce, salmon, and cherry tomatoes in a bowl.
➢ Wash and dry the lemon and grate the zest into the bowl with the salmon.
➢ Strain the juice into another bowl and add salt, pepper, oil, and chives. Stir until you get a smooth sauce.
➢ Pour the emulsion over the salad, mix well, and serve.

Shrimp salad with radishes and cucumbers

2 servings I Calories: 220
Nutritional values: carbs: 6 gr; protein: 28 gr; fat: 7 gr

Ingredients
✓ 400 gr of shrimp
✓ 1 cucumber
✓ 1 stalk of celery
✓ 4 radishes
✓ ½ yellow pepper
✓ ½ lemon
✓ Chopped parsley to taste
✓ Salt and pepper to taste
✓ Olive oil to taste

Directions
➢ Shell the shrimps, remove the black filament and wash them under running water.
➢ Heat a little oil in a pan and put the shrimp to cook for 4 minutes.
➢ After 4 minutes, season with salt and pepper, turn off and temporarily set aside.
➢ Wash the cucumber, trim it, and cut it into slices.
➢ Wash the radishes and cut them into rings.
➢ Wash the pepper and cut it into cubes.
➢ Wash the celery and cut it into small pieces.
➢ Put all the vegetables in a bowl. Add the shrimps and season with oil, salt, pepper and lemon juice.
➢ Mix well, sprinkle with chopped parsley and serve.

Spinach, cherry tomatoes, and feta salad

2 servings I Calories: 272
Nutritional values: carbs: 9 gr; protein: 14 gr; fat: 15 gr

Ingredients
✓ 250 gr of cherry tomatoes
✓ 100 gr of spinach
✓ 50 gr of rocket salad
✓ 100 gr of feta cheese
✓ ½ red onion
✓ ½ lemon
✓ Salt and pepper to taste
✓ Olive oil to taste

Directions

- ➤ Wash and dry the spinach, cut them into strips and then cook them for 5 minutes in a pan with hot oil.
- ➤ Wash the cherry tomatoes and then cut them in half.
- ➤ Wash and dry the rocket.
- ➤ Peel and cut the red onion into slices.
- ➤ Put all the ingredients in a bowl. Add the feta cut into cubes.
- ➤ Add the lemon juice, salt, pepper, and olive oil.
- ➤ Mix well and serve the salad.

Soups

Avocado soup

2 servings | Calories: 226
Nutritional values: carbs: 6 gr; protein: 4 gr; fat: 18 gr

Ingredients
- ✓ 2 avocados
- ✓ 65 gr of Greek yoghurt
- ✓ ½ lemon
- ✓ 300 ml of hot chicken broth
- ✓ Chopped chives to taste
- ✓ Salt and pepper to taste
- ✓ Olive oil to taste

Directions
- ➤ Peel the avocados, remove the stone, and then cut them into small pieces. Put the avocados in a bowl and sprinkle them with the lemon juice.
- ➤ Put the avocado in the blender and add the yoghurt, salt and pepper and the broth. Operate the blender and blend until you get a creamy mixture.
- ➤ Put the mixture in a bowl, cover the bowl with cling film and refrigerate to rest for 30 minutes.
- ➤ After 30 minutes, take the bowl and divide the avocado soup into two bowls.
- ➤ Sprinkle the soup with chives and a drizzle of olive oil and serve.

Coconut mussel soup

2 servings | Calories: 326
Nutritional values: carbs: 5 gr; protein: 26 gr; fat: 22 gr

Ingredients
- ✓ 700 gr of mussels already cleaned
- ✓ 130 ml of fish broth
- ✓ 1 tbsp of curry powder
- ✓ 2 tsp of fish sauce
- ✓ 250 ml of coconut milk
- ✓ 3 tsp of chopped fresh cilantro
- ✓ Salt and pepper to taste

Directions
- ➤ Put the fish broth in a saucepan and bring to a boil.
- ➤ Add the fish sauce and curry powder and cook for 2 minutes.
- ➤ Rinse the mussels under running water and put them in the pot with the broth. Cook for 1 minute and then add the coconut milk.
- ➤ Season with salt and pepper, cover the pot with the lid and cook for another 8 minutes.
- ➤ As soon as the soup is cooked, turn it off and divide it into two plates.
- ➤ Sprinkle with chopped cilantro and serve.

Curry fish soup

2 servings | Calories: 411
Nutritional values: carbs: 9 gr; protein: 22 gr; fat: 31 gr

Ingredients
- ✓ 250 gr of cod fillets
- ✓ ½ tbsp of fish sauce
- ✓ ½ lime
- ✓ 175 ml of coconut milk
- ✓ 1 tbsp of chopped cilantro
- ✓ 2 tbsp of curry paste or curry powder

✓ 125 ml of coconut cream
✓ Olive oil to taste
✓ Salt and pepper to taste

Directions

➢ Wash the cod fillet, remove the skin and bones, and then cut it into smaller fillets.
➢ Pour some oil into the wok or pan and let it heat up.
➢ Once it is hot, add the curry paste. Mix well and cook for 3 minutes.
➢ Add the coconut milk and fish sauce and cook for another 8 minutes.
➢ Now add the cod fillets and cook for 4 minutes per side.
➢ Now add the coconut cream, coriander, and lime juice, season with salt and pepper and cook for another 2 minutes.
➢ When cooked, turn off, put the curry fish soup on two plates and serve.

Egg and thyme soup

2 servings I Calories: 146
Nutritional values: carbs: 2 gr; protein: 16 gr; fat: 8 gr

Ingredients
✓ 2 eggs
✓ 2 sprigs of thyme
✓ 1 clove of garlic
✓ Olive oil to taste
✓ Salt and pepper to taste

Directions

➢ Wash and dry the thyme sprigs.
➢ Peel and chop the garlic clove.
➢ Heat a little olive oil in a pan and then add the garlic and a sprig of thyme.
➢ Fry for 2 minutes and then add 500 ml of water.

➢ Bring to a boil, then add salt and pepper and cook for another 5 minutes.
➢ Meanwhile, separate the yolks from the whites. Put the egg yolks in a cup and add a little oil.
➢ Put the egg whites in another bowl and beat them with a fork.
➢ After 5 minutes, add the egg whites to the broth. Stir, cook for 1 minute and then add the egg yolks.
➢ Stir constantly and cook for another 3 minutes.
➢ After 3 minutes, turn off, divide the soup into two plates and serve.

Fennel soup

2 servings I Calories: 196
Nutritional values: carbs: 4 gr; protein: 7 gr; fat: 16 gr

Ingredients
✓ 450 gr of fennel
✓ 100 ml of vegetable broth
✓ 25 ml of cooking cream
✓ 20 gr of onion
✓ Salt and pepper to taste
✓ Olive oil to taste

Directions

➢ Remove the outer leaves of the fennel, wash them, and then cut them into small pieces.
➢ Peel and chop the onion.
➢ Heat some olive oil in a pan and add the onion.
➢ Sauté for 5 minutes and then add the fennel. Cook for 8 minutes, then add salt, pepper, and the vegetable broth.
➢ Cook for another 10 minutes, then lower the heat and blend everything with an immersion blender.

➢ Now add the cooking cream and let it thicken for another 5 minutes, stirring constantly.

➢ As soon as the soup is ready, put it on plates, season with a drizzle of oil and serve.

Ginger chicken soup

2 servings I Calories: 276
Nutritional values: carbs: 7 gr; protein: 24 gr; fat: 10 gr

Ingredients
- ✓ 250 gr of chicken breast
- ✓ 600 ml of hot chicken broth
- ✓ 2 tsp of grated fresh ginger
- ✓ 200 gr of pumpkin pulp
- ✓ 1 tbsp of soy sauce
- ✓ Salt and pepper to taste

Directions
➢ Remove the fat from the chicken breast and then cut it in small cubes.

➢ Wash the pumpkin pulp and cut it into small cubes.

➢ Put the chicken, ginger, salt, pepper, and broth in a saucepan and cook for 10 minutes.

➢ After 10 minutes, remove the chicken and add the pumpkin cubes and soy sauce.

➢ Cook for another 10 minutes and then turn off.

➢ Place the chicken on two plates.

➢ Pour over the broth and serve.

Pumpkin soup

2 servings I Calories: 213
Nutritional values: carbs: 11 gr; protein: 9 gr; fat: 10 gr

Ingredients
- ✓ 300 gr of pumpkin pulp
- ✓ 300 ml of milk
- ✓ 150 ml of water
- ✓ 50 gr of grated parmesan cheese
- ✓ Salt and pepper to taste
- ✓ Olive oil to taste

Directions
➢ Wash the pumpkin pulp and then cut it into cubes of about 3 cm.

➢ Put the pumpkin in a pan, add salt, pepper, and water, put the lid on and cook for 10 minutes.

➢ Add the milk, and cook for another 10 minutes, stirring often.

➢ After 10 minutes, turn off and with an immersion blender blend everything until you get a creamy mixture.

➢ Add the parmesan and stir until completely dissolved.

➢ Put the pumpkin soup on the plates, season it with a drizzle of oil and serve.

Scrambled egg soup

2 servings I Calories: 334
Nutritional values: carbs: 1 gr; protein: 12 gr; fat: 14 gr

Ingredients
- ✓ 500 ml of meat broth
- ✓ 4 eggs
- ✓ 40 gr of grated parmesan cheese
- ✓ A pinch of nutmeg
- ✓ Chopped parsley to taste
- ✓ Salt and pepper to taste
- ✓ Olive oil to taste

Directions
➢ Pour the meat broth into a saucepan and bring it to a boil.

> Break the eggs into a bowl. Add salt, pepper, nutmeg, parmesan, and parsley. Beat the eggs with a fork until you get a homogeneous mixture.
> Pour the mixture into the pot with the boiling broth and mix continuously with a hand whisk for 5 minutes.
> After 5 minutes turn off, put the scrambled egg soup on the plates, season with a drizzle of oil and serve.

Zucchini and avocado soup

2 servings I Calories: 309
Nutritional values: carbs: 10 gr; protein: 8 gr; fat: 18 gr

Ingredients
✓ 200 gr of courgettes
✓ 10 gr of flaked almonds
✓ 2 spring onion 1
✓ 1 tsp of minced ginger
✓ 250 gr of avocado
✓ ½ lemon
✓ 1 tbsp of chopped chives
✓ 75 gr of cherry tomatoes
✓ 30 gr of black olives
✓ Olive oil to taste
✓ Salt and pepper to taste

Directions
> Peel and wash the courgettes, wash them, and cut them into cubes.
> Peel the spring onions, wash them, and then cut them into slices.
> Peel the avocados, remove the stones, and then cut the pulp into slices. Put the avocado pulp in a bowl and season with the lemon juice.
> Put some oil in a saucepan and let it heat up. Add the spring onions and ginger and brown them for 10 minutes.
> Add the courgettes, add a cup of hot water, season with salt and pepper and cook for another 10 minutes.
> Meanwhile, wash the cherry tomatoes, cut them in half and put them in a bowl. Season with oil, salt, pepper and chopped chives.
> After 10 minutes, turn off and add the avocado to the pot with the courgettes. Take an immersion blender and blend all the ingredients in the pot.
> Put the soup on the plates. Add the cherry tomatoes and olives and serve.

Zucchini, parsley, and basil soup

2 servings I Calories: 220
Nutritional values: carbs: 9 gr; protein: 2 gr; fat: 8 gr

Ingredients
✓ 4 courgettes
✓ 1 onion
✓ 1 clove of garlic
✓ 6 basil leaves
✓ 6 parsley leaves
✓ Salt and pepper to taste
✓ Olive oil to taste

Directions
> Trim the courgettes. Wash the courgettes and then cut them into cubes of about 2 cm each.
> Wash and dry the basil and parsley leaves.
> Peel and chop the garlic.
> Peel the onion and then cut it into slices.

- ➢ Heat a drizzle of oil in a pan and then add the garlic and onion. Sauté for 5 minutes and then add the courgettes.
- ➢ Season with salt and pepper, add a cup of water and bring to a boil. Cook for another 5 minutes and then turn off.
- ➢ Add the parsley, basil, and garlic. Take an immersion blender and blend until thick and creamy.
- ➢ Put the soup on the plates, season it with a drizzle of oil and serve.

Snacks

Avocado, almond and yoghurt smoothie

2 servings I Calories: 202
Nutritional values: carbs: 8 gr; protein: 6 gr; fat: 13 gr

Ingredients
- ✓ 2 small ripe avocados
- ✓ 300 ml of unsweetened almond milk
- ✓ 1 tbsp of stevia powder
- ✓ 300 gr of frozen Greek yoghurt
- ✓ 10 shelled almonds

Directions
- ➤ Peel the avocados, remove the stones, cut the pulp into pieces, and then put it in the glass of the blender.
- ➤ Add the stevia, almond milk, almonds, and Greek yoghurt.
- ➤ Operate the blender and blend until you get a homogeneous and creamy mixture.
- ➤ Pour the smoothie into two glasses and serve.

Chocolate and peanut butter smoothie

2 servings I Calories: 364
Nutritional values: carbs: 12 gr; protein: 25 gr; fat: 12 gr

Ingredients
- ✓ 480 ml of unsweetened almond milk
- ✓ 60 grams of peanut butter
- ✓ 2 tbsp of unsweetened cocoa powder
- ✓ 8 ice cubes
- ✓ 2 tbsp of whipping cream

Directions
- ➤ Put the almond milk, peanut butter, cocoa and whipping cream in the blender glass.
- ➤ Blend for 30 seconds and then add the ice.
- ➤ Blend for a minute, then pour the smoothie into two glasses and serve.

Chunks of salmon and bacon

2 servings I Calories: 419
Nutritional values: carbs: 1 gr; protein: 39 gr; fat: 27 gr

Ingredients
- ✓ 350 gr of salmon fillet
- ✓ 75 gr of sliced bacon
- ✓ Sage to taste
- ✓ Salt and pepper to taste

Directions
- ➤ Wash the salmon fillet, dry it, and remove the skin and bones. Cut the salmon into cubes of about 2 cm each.
- ➤ Wash and dry the sage leaves.
- ➤ Season the salmon with salt and pepper and then wrap it in sage leaves and slices of bacon.
- ➤ Keep each slice of bacon closed on the morsel with a wooden toothpick and place the salmon morsels on a lightly buttered baking pan.

> Put in the oven and cook for 12 minutes at 200 ° c, turning them from time to time.
> Once cooked, take the morsels from the oven, place them on plates and serve.

Endive leaves stuffed with tuna

2 servings I Calories: 146
Nutritional values: carbs: 2 gr; protein: 13 gr; fat: 10 gr

Ingredients
- ✓ 50 gr of drained tuna in oil
- ✓ 50 gr of fresh spreadable cheese
- ✓ ½ lemon
- ✓ 6 belgian endive leaves
- ✓ Chopped parsley to taste
- ✓ Salt and pepper to taste

Directions
> Drain the tuna and put it in a bowl.
> Mash the tuna with a fork and add the cheese, lemon juice, parsley, salt, and pepper. Stir until you get a homogeneous mixture.
> Wash and dry the endive leaves and place them in a serving dish.
> Fill the endive leaves with the tuna mixture, put on the table and serve.

Mint, blackberry, and coconut smoothie

2 servings I Calories: 153
Nutritional values: carbs: 8 gr; protein: 11 gr; fat: 6 gr

Ingredients
- ✓ 240 ml unsweetened coconut milk
- ✓ 140 gr of blackberries
- ✓ 40 gr of grated coconut
- ✓ 20 mint leaves
- ✓ 6 ice cubes

Directions
> Wash and dry the blackberries and put them in the blender glass.
> Wash and dry the mint leaves and put them in the blender.
> Add the grated coconut, coconut milk and ice.
> Operate the blender and blend until you get a thick and homogeneous mixture.
> Pour the smoothie into two glasses and serve.

Raspberry and cinnamon smoothie

2 servings I Calories: 164
Nutritional values: carb: 11 gr; protein: 6 gr; fat: 6 gr

Ingredients
- ✓ 480 ml of unsweetened almond milk
- ✓ 200 gr of raspberries
- ✓ 40 gr of spinach
- ✓ 1 tsp of cinnamon powder
- ✓ 200 grams of frozen Greek yoghurt

Directions
> Wash and dry the raspberries and put them inside the blender.
> Wash the spinach, dry them, and put them in the blender.
> Add the almond milk and cinnamon and blend for 30 seconds.
> Now add the Greek yoghurt and blend until you get a creamy and thick mixture.
> Pour the smoothie into two glasses and serve.

Strawberry and mint avocado smoothie

2 servings I Calories: 207
Nutritional values: carbs: 10 gr; protein: 5 gr; fat: 16 gr

Ingredients
- ✓ 1 avocado
- ✓ 12 strawberries
- ✓ 10 mint leaves
- ✓ ½ lime
- ✓ 150 grams of frozen Greek yoghurt
- ✓ 150 ml of unsweetened coconut milk

Directions
- ➢ Wash the strawberries and cut them in half.
- ➢ Peel the avocado, remove the stone, and then cut it into cubes.
- ➢ Wash the mint leaves.
- ➢ Wash the lime and remove the zest.
- ➢ Put the strawberries, avocado, lime zest, mint leaves, and coconut milk in the blender.
- ➢ Blend for 1 minute and then add the Greek yoghurt.
- ➢ Blend again for 1 minute, then turn off, pour the smoothie into two glasses, and serve.

Strawberry lassi

2 servings I Calories: 187
Nutritional values: carbs: 7 gr; protein: 8 gr; fat: 18 gr

Ingredients
- ✓ 330 gr of strawberries
- ✓ 300 gr of Greek yoghurt
- ✓ 1 tsp of stevia powder
- ✓ 100 ml of unsweetened almond milk

Directions
- ➢ Wash and dry the strawberries and then cut them in half.
- ➢ Put the strawberries in the blender and add the yoghurt and stevia.
- ➢ Blend for 1 minute and then add the almond milk.
- ➢ Blend until you get a thick and creamy mixture.
- ➢ Pour the lassi into two glasses and serve.

Strawberry and berry smoothie

2 servings I Calories: 186
Nutritional values: carbs: 10 gr; protein: 5 gr; fat: 7 gr

Ingredients
- ✓ 180 gr of strawberries
- ✓ 180 gr of raspberries
- ✓ 120 gr of blackberries
- ✓ 240 ml unsweetened coconut milk
- ✓ 6 ice cubes
- ✓ Coconut flakes to taste

Directions
- ➢ Wash and dry strawberries, raspberries, and blackberries.
- ➢ Put the fruit in the blender glass.
- ➢ Add the ice and coconut milk and blend until you get a creamy mixture.
- ➢ Pour the smoothie into two glasses, sprinkle with coconut and serve.

Tomatoes stuffed with tuna, cheese, and olives

2 servings I Calories: 355
Nutritional values: carbs: 9 gr; protein: 31 gr; fat: 19 gr

Ingredients
- ✓ 2 ripe red tomatoes
- ✓ 75 gr of fresh spreadable cheese
- ✓ 2 tsp of chopped thyme
- ✓ 180 grams of tuna in oil
- ✓ 10 pitted black olives
- ✓ Salt and pepper to taste
- ✓ Olive oil to taste

Directions
- ➢ Wash and dry the tomatoes, remove the top and empty the inside with the help of a spoon.
- ➢ Put the tomato pulp in a bowl and season with salt and pepper.
- ➢ Stir and then add the drained tuna, cheese, thyme, and black olives cut into small pieces.
- ➢ Put the tomatoes on two plates and fill them with the tuna filling.
- ➢ Season everything with a drizzle of oil and serve.

Desserts

Almonds and yoghurt dessert

2 servings I Calories: 220
Nutritional values: carbs: 9 gr; protein: 8 gr; fat: 15 gr

Ingredients
- ✓ 100 gr of almond flour
- ✓ 2 eggs
- ✓ ½ glass of sugar-free almond milk
- ✓ 50 gr of melted butter (or melted coconut oil)
- ✓ 30 gr of powdered stevia
- ✓ 70 gr of Greek yoghurt
- ✓ 1 tbsp of baking powder
- ✓ 1 pinch of salt

Directions
- ➢ First preheat the oven to 210° c.
- ➢ Put the stevia in a mixer and let it pulverize for 10 seconds at maximum speed.
- ➢ It must become the consistency of a sort of icing sugar.
- ➢ Add the powdered stevia with the 2 eggs to a bowl and beat them for some minute.
- ➢ Once the eggs have become frothy, add the almond flour, yoghurt, melted butter, almond milk and mix with a wooden spoon or spatula.
- ➢ Finally add the baking powder by passing it through a sieve and blend well with the other ingredients.

- ➢ Pour the mixture into a greased suitable little mold.
- ➢ Cook for about 10/15 minutes.
- ➢ Serve the almond and yoghurt cake as dessert when it has cooled.

Avocado and raspberry skewers

2 servings I Calories: 160
Nutritional values: carbs: 7 gr; protein: 4 gr; fat: 13 gr

Ingredients
- ✓ 1 little avocado
- ✓ 80 grams of raspberries
- ✓ 1 lime
- ✓ 1 tsp of stevia
- ✓ Olive oil to taste
- ✓ Salt and pepper to taste

Directions
- ➢ Start with peeling avocado. Halve it, remove the central stone, and cut avocado pulp and then cut it into small cubes.
- ➢ Take the raspberries, wash, and dry them, leaving whole.
- ➢ At this point, take a skewer and put first a cube of avocado and then some raspberries. Keep on this way until you have used up all the fruits.
- ➢ In the meantime, wash and dry the lime and take the zest. Put the lime zest in a bowl with oil, salt, stevia, pepper and mix well.
- ➢ Sprinkle the avocado and raspberries skewers with the lime emulsion, put them on serving plates and serve.

Blackberry and almond salad

2 servings I Calories: 100
Nutritional values: carbs: 7 gr;
protein: 5 gr; fat: 8 gr

Ingredients
- ✓ 200 gr of blackberries
- ✓ 2 limes
- ✓ 40 gr of sliced almonds
- ✓ 1 tsp of ginger powder

Directions
- ➢ First, wash the blackberries and then cut into pieces.
- ➢ Put blackberries in a large bowl and season with the lime juice. Add the sliced almonds as well.
- ➢ Sprinkle your blackberry salad with ginger, leave to flavour for 30 minutes about and then put the fruit salad in serving bowls and serve your keto dessert.

Blueberry and peanuts smoothie

2 servings I Calories for servings: 120
Nutritional values: carbs: 6 gr;
protein: 3 gr; fat: 10 gr

Ingredients
- ✓ 50 gr of blueberries
- ✓ 40 gr of Greek yoghurt
- ✓ 1 tsp of cinnamon
- ✓ 40 gr of ice
- ✓ 20 gr of peanuts
- ✓ 60 ml of unsweetened soy milk

Directions
- ➢ First, wash the blueberries well under running water, dry them and put them in the mixer.
- ➢ Add the rest of the ingredients to the mixer and blend everything at maximum speed.
- ➢ Stir with a spatula and pour the smoothie into a glass.Serve it immediately.

Chocolate panna cotta

2 servings I Calories: 170
Nutritional values: carbs: 6 gr; protein: 4 gr; fat: 14 gr

Ingredients
- ✓ 200 ml of sugar free almond milk
- ✓ 10 gr of low-carb instant gelatine powder
- ✓ 20 gr of chopped (90% of cocoa) chocolate
- ✓ 10 gr of powdered stevia
- ✓ 1 vanilla pod

Directions
- ➢ You can start by putting the gelatine to soak in cold water for 10 minutes.
- ➢ Meanwhile, put half of the almond milk in a saucepan along with the stevia and chopped chocolate.
- ➢ Leave a little milk to one side to mix the gelatine later.
- ➢ Heat over low heat, stirring constantly.
- ➢ Once the cream comes to a boil, remove it from the heat and add the instant gelatine powder.
- ➢ Also add vanilla pod and mix well.
- ➢ Before it comes to a boil, remove from heat.
- ➢ Add the rest of the almond milk that you had set aside, and mix well, to mix the jelly.
- ➢ Pour the panna cotta into 2 aluminium cups and put it to rest in the fridge for at least 6 hours.

➢ As soon as it is time to serve the panna cotta, put very hot water in a container and immerse the bottom of the cups for a few seconds.
➢ Then take them and turn them upside down on a serving dish.
➢ You can serve.

Coconut vanilla and strawberry sorbet

2 servings I Calories: 90
Nutritional values: carbs: 6 gr; protein: 0 gr; fat: 8 gr

Ingredients
✓ 100 grams of strawberries
✓ 1 tbsp of vanilla extract
✓ 30 grams of melted coconut oil
✓ 1 cup of ice
✓ 1 tbsp of coconut flour

Directions
➢ Firs, wash strawberries and let them dry. Cut into pieces
➢ Put the strawberry pieces, vanilla, and melted coconut oil in the blender glass.
➢ Mix all ingredients at high speed for one minute about.
➢ Now add the ice and blend until you will obtain a homogeneous and coloured mixture.
➢ Put the strawberry and coconut sorbet in the glasses, decorate with the coconut flour and serve.

Cream cheese cranberry and vanilla mousse

2 servings I Calories :130
Nutritional values: carbs: 4 gr; protein: 7 gr; fat: 12 gr

Ingredients
✓ 120 gr of fresh cream cheese
✓ 1 glass of water
✓ 1 tbsp of vanilla extract
✓ 1 cup of chopped cranberries
✓ 1 tsp of liquid stevia
✓ 20 grams of chopped pistachios

Directions
➢ Start the recipe by washing and drying the cranberries, then chop. Put cranberries pieces and a glass of water in the saucepan and cook them with the stevia until you have obtained a sort of red syrup.
➢ Put the cream cheese in a bowl and add the vanilla and chopped pistachios.
➢ Stir and mix well and then add the cranberry syrup.
➢ With the help of a manual whisk, mix all the ingredients until you have obtained a smooth and compact dough.
➢ Put the cream cheese and cranberry mousse in the glasses and keep it in the fridge until you will be ready to serve it.

Pecans and cocoa pudding

2 servings I Calories:150
Nutritional values: carbs: 7 gr; protein: 6 gr; fat: 12 gr

Ingredients
✓ 60 gr of coconut flour
✓ 40 gr of sugar free cocoa powder
✓ 30 gr of chopped pecans
✓ 100 ml of water
✓ 2 tbsp of sugar free soy milk
✓ 2 tbsp of Greek yoghurt

Directions

➢ Fist, take the Greek yoghurt and put it in a microwave-safe bowl.
➢ After that add coconut flour, water, soy milk and cocoa powder.
➢ Let microwave for 40 seconds about.
➢ After 40 seconds add pecans and microwave for another 25/30 seconds.
➢ Once it's ready you can serve this very easy pudding.

Spinach avocado and red fruits smoothie

2 servings I Calories:110
Nutritional values: carbs: 4 gr; protein: 6 gr; fat: 12 gr

Ingredients
✓ 120 ml of sugar free soy milk
✓ 50 gr of fresh spinach leaves
✓ 60 gr of red fruits
✓ 30 gr of ice
✓ 80 gr of avocado pulp

Preparation
➢ First, wash and dry the red fruits.
➢ Put the avocado pulp cut into pieces, the red fruits, and the soy milk in the bowl of the mixer.
➢ Wash and dry the spinach and then mix it with the other ingredients.
➢ Blend all the ingredients together with the blender on high speed.
➢ When the mixture is homogeneous and well blended, turn off the mixer, mix everything with a spatula or a wooden spoon and distribute the smoothie in a glass.
➢ Serve it with a few more red fruits for decoration.

Walnuts almond and coconut cream filled avocado

2 servings I Calories: 260
Nutritional values: carbs: 7 gr; protein: 9 gr fat: 22 gr

Ingredients
• 2 ripe avocados
• 30 gr of melted coconut oil
• 30 gr of almond flour
• 20 gr of powdered stevia
• 60 gr of chopped walnuts
• Salt to taste

Directions
1. First, take avocados, cut them in half and remove all central stones, scooping each half avocado very lightly with a teaspoon.
2. Oil a baking dish and arrange the avocados, with the rounded part resting on the bottom of the container. Put the melted coconut oil in a bowl, together with the stevia, almond flour, and a pinch of salt. Work the ingredients for a bit of time, until you get a soft and quite fluffy cream.
3. Chop the walnuts and add them to the coconut and almond cream.
4. Now, divide the coconut and walnuts mixture into equal parts and distribute it in the avocado halves.
5. Place in the oven at 200°c and cook for 10 minutes about.
6. Take the avocados, when cooked, out of the oven and let cool, then serve as dessert.

21 days meal plan

Here is a 21-day food plan for an excellent keto diet. We want to remind you that lunch and dinner can be interchanged.

For what about snacks, you can have 2 (in the morning and in the afternoon) you can choose:

✓ 30 gr of dried fruits
✓ ½ avocado
✓ 150 gr of Greek yoghurt
✓ 30 gr of parmesan cheese
✓ 20 gr of extra dark chocolate (only twice a week)
✓ 100 gr of red fruits (only twice a week)
✓ 1 snack from the recipes

Instead of the lunch or dinner recipes you can choose:

✓ 200 gr of white meat (chicken, pork, turkey)
✓ 150/200 gr of beef (maximum three times a week)
✓ 150 gr of cheese
✓ 150 gr of canned tuna
✓ 150 gr of smoked salmon
✓ 200 gr of cod haddock or plaice or similar white fish

These dishes must be accompanied by a plate of vegetables (green leafy vegetables only).

	Breakfast	Lunch	Dinner
Day 1	A cup of green tea, or a cup of coffee with no sugar and 1 recipe from breakfast recipes	1 salad from the recipes and a big portion of vegetables	1 main course from the recipes (or a fish or a salad recipe) and a vegetable dish (or a big portion of vegetables)
Day 2	A cup of green tea, or a cup of coffee with no sugar and 1 recipe from breakfast recipes	1 main course from the recipes (or a salad recipe) and a big portion of vegetables	1 main course from the recipes (or a salad recipe) and a big portion of vegetables
Day 3	A cup of green tea, or a cup of coffee with no sugar and 1 recipe from breakfast recipes	1 soup from the recipes and a big portion of vegetables)	1 main course from the recipes (or a salad recipe) and a big portion of vegetables
Day 4	A cup of green tea, two wholemeal rusks, a seasonal fruit	1 soup from the recipes	1 main course from the recipes (or a salad recipe) and a big portion of

			vegetables
Day 5	A cup of green tea, or a cup of coffee with no sugar and 1 recipe from breakfast recipes	1 salad dish 100 grams of red fruits	1 main course from the recipes (or a salad recipe) and a big portion of vegetables
Day 6	A cup of green tea, or a cup of coffee with no sugar and 1 recipe from breakfast recipes	1 soup from the recipes and a big portion of vegetables	1 main course from the recipes and a big portion of vegetables
Day 7	A cup of green tea, or a cup of coffee with no sugar and 1 recipe from breakfast recipes	1 main course from the recipes	1 main course from the recipes and a big portion of vegetables
Day 7	A cup of green tea, or a cup of coffee with no sugar and 1 recipe from breakfast recipes	1 main course from the recipe and big portion of vegetables	1 soup from the recipe and 200 grams of green vegetables
Day 8	A cup of green tea, or a cup of coffee with no sugar and 1 recipe from breakfast recipes	1 salad dish and 40 grams of dried fruits	1 main course from the recipes
Day 9	A cup of green tea, or a cup of coffee with no sugar and 1 recipe from breakfast recipes	1 main course from the recipes and a big portion of vegetables	1 main course from the recipes and a soup
Day 10	A coffee without sugar, a cup of vegetable milk, 2 keto biscuits	1 main course from the recipes and a big portion of vegetables	1 salad dish from recipes
Day 11	A cup of green tea, or a cup of coffee with no sugar and 1 recipe from breakfast recipes	1 main course from the recipes and a big portion of vegetables	1 main course from the recipes and a big portion of vegetables
Day 12	A coffee without sugar, a cup of vegetable milk, 2 keto biscuits	1 main course from the recipes	1 soup from the recipes and 100 grams of tuna in oil
Day 13	A cup of green tea, or a cup of coffee with no sugar and 1 recipe from breakfast recipes	1 main course from the recipes and a big portion of vegetables	1 salad recipe
Day 14	A cup of green tea, or a cup of coffee with no sugar and 1 recipe from breakfast recipes	1 main course from the recipes and a big portion of vegetables	1 soup recipe and 100 grams of strawberries
Day 15	A cup of green tea, and 1 recipe from breakfast recipes	1 main course from the recipes and a big portion of vegetables	1 main course from the recipes and a big portion of vegetables
Day 16	A cup of green tea, or a cup of coffee with no sugar and 1 recipe from breakfast recipes	1 soup recipe and a big portion of vegetables	1 main course from the recipes and a big portion of vegetables
Day 17	A cup of green tea, or a cup of coffee with no sugar and 1 recipe from breakfast recipes	1 main course from the recipes and a big portion of vegetables	1 salad recipe and 1 soup recipe
Day 18	A coffee without sugar, a cup of vegetable milk, 2 keto biscuits	1 main course from the recipes and a big portion of vegetables	1 main course from the recipes
Day 19	A cup of green tea, or a cup of coffee with no sugar and 1 recipe from breakfast recipes	1 main course from the recipes and a big portion of vegetables	1 main course from the recipes and a big portion of vegetables

Day 20	A coffee without sugar, a cup of vegetable milk, 2 keto biscuits	1 salad recipe and ½ avocado	1 main course from the recipes and a big portion of vegetables
Day 21	A cup of green tea, or a cup of coffee with no sugar and 1 recipe from breakfast recipes	1 main course from the recipes and a big portion of vegetables	1 main course from the recipe and 1 soup recipe

Printed in Great Britain
by Amazon

31586955R00037